Wood-Ridge Memorial Library

231 Hackensack Street
Wood-Ridge, NJ 07075

DEFINING MOMENTS
THE WPA—
PUTTING AMERICA
TO WORK

DEFINING MOMENTS
THE WPA—
PUTTING AMERICA
TO WORK

Jeff Hill

155 W. Congress, Suite 200
Detroit, MI 48226

Omnigraphics, Inc.

Kevin Hillstrom, *Series Editor*
Cherie D. Abbey, *Managing Editor*

Peter E. Ruffner, *Publisher*
Matthew P. Barbour, *Senior Vice President*

Elizabeth Collins, *Research and Permissions Coordinator*
Kevin M. Hayes, *Operations Manager*

Mary Butler, *Researcher*
Shirley Amore, Joseph Harris, Martha Johns, and Kirk Kauffmann, *Administrative Staff*

Copyright © 2014 Omnigraphics, Inc.
ISBN 978-0-7808-1331-1

Library of Congress Cataloging-in-Publication Data

Hill, Jeff, 1962-
    The WPA—putting America to work / by Jeff Hill.
      pages cm. — (Defining moments)
    Includes bibliographical references and index.
    Summary: "Provides users with a detailed and authoritative overview of the Works Progress Administration (WPA), the centerpiece of the New Deal programs put in place by President Franklin D. Roosevelt to tame the Great Depression and get America back on its feet. Includes biographies, primary sources, and more"— Provided by publisher.
    Audience: Grade 9 to 12.
    ISBN 978-0-7808-1331-1 (hardcover : alk. paper) 1. United States. Work Projects Administration—History—Juvenile literature. 2. Unemployment—United States—History—20th century—Juvenile literature. 3. Manpower policy—United States—History—20th century—Juvenile literature. 4. Public service employment—United States—History—20th century—Juvenile literature. 5. New Deal, 1933-1939—Juvenile literature. 6. Depressions—1929—United States—Juvenile literature. 7. United States—Economic conditions—1918-1945—Juvenile literature. I. Title.
    HD5713.6.U54H54 2013
    362.5'84—dc23   2013022479

The information in this publication was compiled from sources cited and from sources considered reliable. While every possible effort has been made to ensure reliability, the publisher will not assume liability for damages caused by inaccuracies in the data, and makes no warranty, express or implied, on the accuracy of the information contained herein.

This book is printed on acid-free paper meeting the ANSI Z39.48 Standard. The infinity symbol that appears above indicates that the paper in this book meets that standard.

Printed in the United States of America

TABLE OF CONTENTS

NARRATIVE OVERVIEW

BIOGRAPHIES

PRIMARY SOURCES

PREFACE

Throughout the course of America's existence, its people, culture, and institutions have been periodically challenged—and in many cases transformed—by profound historical events. Some of these momentous events, such as women's suffrage, the civil rights movement, and U.S. involvement in World War II, invigorated the nation and strengthened American confidence and capabilities. Others, such as the Great Depression, the Vietnam War, and Watergate, have prompted troubled assessments and heated debates about the country's core beliefs and character.

Some of these defining moments in American history were years or even decades in the making. The Harlem Renaissance and the New Deal, for example, unfurled over the span of several years, while the American labor movement and the Cold War evolved over the course of decades. Other defining moments, such as the Cuban missile crisis and the Japanese attack on Pearl Harbor, transpired over a matter of days or weeks.

But although significant differences exist among these events in terms of their duration and their place in the timeline of American history, all share the same basic characteristic: they transformed the United States' political, cultural, and social landscape for future generations of Americans.

Taking heed of this fundamental reality, American citizens, schools, and other institutions are increasingly emphasizing the importance of understanding our nation's history. Omnigraphics' *Defining Moments* series was created for the express purpose of meeting this growing appetite for authoritative, useful historical resources. This series will be of enduring value to anyone interested in learning more about America's past—and in understanding how those historical events continue to reverberate in the twenty-first century.

Each individual volume of *Defining Moments* provides a valuable resource for readers interested in learning about the most profound events in our nation's history. Each volume is organized into three distinct sections—Narrative Overview, Biographies, and Primary Sources.

- The **Narrative Overview** provides readers with a detailed, factual account of the origins and progression of the "defining moment" being examined. It also explores the event's lasting impact on America's political and cultural landscape.

- The **Biographies** section provides valuable biographical background on leading figures associated with the event in question. Each biography concludes with a list of sources for further information on the profiled individual.

- The **Primary Sources** section collects a wide variety of pertinent primary source materials from the era under discussion, including official documents, papers and resolutions, letters, oral histories, memoirs, editorials, and other important works.

Individually, each of these sections is a rich resource for users. Together, they comprise an authoritative, balanced, and absorbing examination of some of the most significant events in U.S. history.

Other notable features contained within each volume in the series include a glossary of important individuals, places, and terms; a detailed chronology featuring page references to relevant sections of the narrative; an annotated bibliography of sources for further study; an extensive general bibliography that reflects the wide range of historical sources consulted by the author; and a subject index.

New Feature—Research Topics for Student Reports

Each volume in the *Defining Moments* series now includes a list of potential research topics for students. Students working on historical research and writing assignments will find this feature especially useful in assessing their options.

Information on the highlighted research topics can be found throughout the different sections of the book—and especially in the narrative overview, biography, and primary source sections. This wide coverage gives readers the flexibility to study the topic through multiple entry points.

Acknowledgements

This series was developed in consultation with a distinguished Advisory Board comprised of public librarians, school librarians, and educators. They evaluated the series as it developed, and their comments and suggestions were invaluable throughout the production process. Any errors in this and other volumes in the series are ours alone. Following is a list of board members who contributed to the *Defining Moments* series:

Comments and Suggestions

We welcome your comments on *Defining Moments: The WPA—Putting America to Work* and suggestions for other events in U.S. history that warrant treatment in the *Defining Moments* series. Correspondence should be addressed to:

Editor, *Defining Moments*
Omnigraphics, Inc.
155 West Congress, Suite 200
Detroit, MI 48236
E-mail: editorial@omnigraphics.com

HOW TO USE THIS BOOK

Defining Moments: The WPA—Putting America to Work provides users with a detailed and authoritative overview of the Works Progress Administration (WPA), the centerpiece of the New Deal programs put in place by President Franklin D. Roosevelt to tame the Great Depression and get America back on its feet again. The preparation and arrangement of this volume—and all other books in the *Defining Moments* series—reflect an emphasis on providing a thorough and objective account of the people and events that have shaped our nation, presented in an easy-to-use reference work.

The WPA—Putting America to Work is divided into three main sections. The first of these sections, **Narrative Overview**, details the impact of the Great Depression on the American people, the response of the Hoover administration to the crisis, and the early relief programs of the New Deal era. It then moves on to explain the origins, mission, and operations of the Works Progress Administration, as well as its emergence as a flashpoint in the nation's political battles of the late 1930s and early 1940s. Finally, it examines the legacy of the WPA on American politics and culture.

The second section, **Biographies**, provides valuable biographical background on American officials and lawmakers closely associated with the WPA. Featured individuals include President Franklin D. Roosevelt; WPA director Harry Hopkins; civil rights icon and WPA administrator Mary McLeod Bethune; Ellen S. Woodward, who directed the WPA's Women's Division; and Orson Welles, the legendary film director and veteran of the WPA's Federal Theatre Project.

The third section, **Primary Sources**, collects essential and illuminating documents on the WPA and its efforts to relieve the devastating effects of the Depression. Featured primary sources include a speech from President Roosevelt extolling the benefits of the WPA; a description of Harry Hopkins's philosophy of work relief by one of his colleagues; recollections of WPA work from men and women who joined the agency's payroll; a firsthand account of the Federal Theatre Project's staging of *The Cradle Will Rock;* and a critique of the WPA by former president Herbert Hoover.

Other valuable features in *The WPA—Putting America to Work* include the following:

- Attribution and referencing of primary sources and other quoted material to help guide users to other valuable historical research resources.
- Glossary of Important People, Places, and Terms.
- A list of potential research topics for further study of the Great Depression, the New Deal, and the Works Progress Administration.
- Detailed Chronology of events with a *see reference* feature. Under this arrangement, events listed in the chronology include a reference to page numbers within the Narrative Overview wherein users can find additional information on the event in question.
- Photographs of the leading figures and major events associated with the New Deal and the Works Progress Administration.
- Sources for Further Study, an annotated list of noteworthy works about the Works Progress Administration, the New Deal, and the Great Depression.
- Extensive bibliography of works consulted in the creation of this book, including books, periodicals, Internet sites, and videotape materials.
- A Subject Index.

RESEARCH TOPICS FOR
DEFINING MOMENTS: THE WPA—PUTTING AMERICA TO WORK

When students receive an assignment to produce a research paper on a historical event or topic, the first step in that process—settling on a subject for the paper—can also be one of the most vexing. In recognition of that reality, each book in the *Defining Moments* series now highlights research areas/topics that receive extensive coverage within that particular volume.

Potential research topics for students using *Defining Moments: WPA—Putting America to Work* include the following:

- The Hoover and Roosevelt administrations took dramatically different approaches to combating the Great Depression. Explain how these policies reflected their respective political philosophies.

- Explain the difference between direct relief and work relief, and discuss reasons why Roosevelt shifted his emphasis from the former to the latter over time.

- During its first two years, the Roosevelt administration established a wide range of new agencies to get Americans back to work and revive the economy. Which one of these agencies would you most liked to have worked for and why?

- WPA director Harry Hopkins said that the agency's first priority was to get Americans back to work and that employing them on "the best possible projects" was a "secondary objective." Explain why you agree or disagree with Hopkins's point of view.

- Conduct research on buildings, bridges, parks, and other public works that were created in your town, region, or state by the WPA during the Depression. Select one and tell the story of its history, answering such questions as: When and where was it built, and how much did it cost?

How did it change the community in which it was built? Is it still currently being used, and what is its general reputation today?

- The WPA instituted a wide range of employment programs specifically designed for musicians, artists, writers, actors, women, and young people. Do you think some of these programs were more worthwhile than others? Did people engaged in artistic careers deserve the same level of assistance as people engaged in more mainstream lines of work? Explain your reasoning.

- Imagine that you are a member of the House Un-American Activities Committee preparing to cross-examine Harry Hopkins. Come up with five questions that you would like to ask him about WPA operations and policies. Now imagine that you are Hopkins, preparing for an appearance before HUAC. Compile five main points that you want to emphasize in your testimony before the committee.

- The U.S. government moved to stop *The Cradle Will Rock* from being performed because it contained controversial political content. Do you think that authorities have the right to take such steps when the art in question is taxpayer funded? Or do such restrictions unduly interfere with artistic and constitutional freedoms? Can you find more recent examples of taxpayer-funded art that generated similar controversies?

NARRATIVE OVERVIEW

PROLOGUE

Many Americans greeted the new year of 1935 in a bleak and uncertain mood. At that point, the country had been struggling with the economic catastrophe of the Great Depression for more than five years. Yet levels of unemployment—and poverty that accompanies the inability to find work—remained extremely high in most parts of the country. Some 11 million Americans who wanted a job still could not find one, and the national unemployment rate hovered in the neighborhood of 22 percent.

The gravity of the situation was not lost on President Franklin D. Roosevelt, who was preparing to deliver his annual message to Congress in the first week of 1935. Since taking office two years before, the president had implemented numerous reforms in hopes of reviving the economy, but conditions had only marginally improved. He had also engineered the passage of new government assistance programs for millions of citizens who had become destitute as a result of the Depression. During his first year in office, for example, Roosevelt had convinced Congress to greatly expand the federal government's role in providing relief assistance. This government aid primarily took the form of direct relief—cash payments and other forms of assistance to qualified individuals or families. These direct relief programs did not impose any work requirements on recipients. By the dawn of 1935, millions of Americans had become dependent on direct relief programs for their continued survival.

Direct relief—which was also known as home relief or, less formally, "the dole"—provided desperate citizens with the means to meet their basic needs for food and shelter. But it also exacted a toll on most of the people who received it. Accepting public assistance was humiliating for men and women who had always supported themselves through their own labor. Many Americans subsequently became overwhelmed by feelings of inadequacy and hopelessness even after direct relief payments removed the threat of homelessness or starvation. A passage from a study of unemployed residents during the Depression summed up the despair and anger that afflicted many citizens who had been forced to accept direct relief to feed their families:

> Mr. Wolf … feels that he is going "nuts" [at not finding employ-ment]. He just keeps walking around town all day long. Mrs. Wolf describes the situation as one in which "nerves are worn thin." She yells at him and he yells back. "Do you think I don't try?" She is sorry after she has yelled at him but sometimes when she is sufficiently miserable, she isn't even sorry. Then she feels malicious enough to want to hurt him, for this is the only out-let she has for her pent-up emotions.[1]

After conducting interviews with dozens of other families who had received direct assistance, the author of the report could offer only the faintest of praise for that form of aid: "All that can be said for Home Relief is that it kept people alive."[2]

Roosevelt agreed with this assessment. Though he had been instrumen-tal in the effort to increase federally funded relief, the president held deep-seated reservations about the dole's impact on America's vitality and spirit. After two years in office, his doubts were as strong as ever. So as he and his advisors pre-pared his annual message for 1935, they pondered new ways to tackle Ameri-ca's deep economic problems. They eventually settled on another form of assistance—work relief—which had been used to a limited degree by federal and state agencies since the early 1930s. Under work relief, aid recipients only received government checks in return for labor on public work projects.

The president and his top advisors believed that work relief programs offered distinct advantages over the dole. Such programs could accomplish use-ful tasks—such as new construction—that would benefit the wider community. They could also help spur economic growth by putting paychecks in the hands of millions of workers. Finally, and perhaps most importantly, gainful employ-ment with the federal government could provide a sense of purpose and pride to individuals who had been reduced to a grim and humbling existence by the Depression.

On January 4, 1935, Roosevelt appeared before a joint session of Congress and made his case for a new federal employment program:

> Continued dependence upon relief induces a spiritual and moral disintegration fundamentally destructive to the national fibre. To dole out relief in this way is to administer a narcotic, a subtle

destroyer of the human spirit. It is inimical to the dictates of sound policy. It is in violation of the traditions of America. Work must be found for able-bodied but destitute workers.

The Federal Government must and shall quit this business of relief.

I am not willing that the vitality of our people be further sapped by the giving of cash, of market baskets, of a few hours of weekly work cutting grass, raking leaves or picking up papers in the public parks. We must preserve not only the bodies of the unemployed from destitution but also their self-respect, their self-reliance and courage and determination....

There are ... three and one half million employable people who are on relief.... This group was the victim of a nation-wide depression caused by conditions which were not local but national. The Federal Government is the only governmental agency with sufficient power and credit to meet this situation.... It is a duty dictated by every intelligent consideration of national policy to ask you to make it possible for the United States to give employment to all of these three and one half million employable people now on relief, pending their absorption in a rising tide of private employment.[3]

Put another way, the president wanted the federal government to stop handing out relief payments and to start handing out jobs—millions of jobs. Moreover, he proposed that the program continue until the victims of the Depression once again found work in the private sector. In essence, Roosevelt asked Congress to create the biggest jobs program in the nation's history.

Three months later, his request became a reality and the Works Progress Administration (WPA) opened its doors. By the end of 1935, the WPA employed a vast army of Americans who had previously struggled to fill the empty hours of their day. They built roads, buildings, and water systems. They cooked lunches for schoolchildren and performed plays for local communities. They sewed sheets for hospitals and taught literacy classes.

But the monumental WPA program also created monumental controversy. Many Americans considered relief employment to be "make-work"—wasteful exercises that accomplished little of use. Others viewed such programs as a dangerous expansion of government power that could threaten private enterprise and personal liberty. Critics also objected to the WPA on the basis of cost, since it required enormous sums of taxpayer money to maintain its operations and pay its work force.

The agency thus became a source of heated debate as soon as soon as President Roosevelt called for its creation. Over the next eight years of WPA operations, that debate never subsided. Instead, politicians, newspaper editors, and neighbors all argued passionately about the WPA's basic mission, its operating practices, and whether it was good for America. All this time, however, the men and women who made up the WPA work force kept showing up for work. And in the process, they changed the United States forever.

Notes

[1] Quoted in Ginzberg, Eli. *The Unemployed.* Edited by Ben B. Seligman. New Brunswick, NJ: Transaction, 2004, p. 74.

[2] Ginzberg, p. 61.

[3] Roosevelt, Franklin D. *The Public Papers and Addresses of Franklin D. Roosevelt, Vol. 4: The Court Disapproves, 1935.* New York: Random House, 1938, pp. 19-21.

Chapter One
A NATION UNEMPLOYED

We shall soon, with the help of God, be in sight of the day when poverty will be banished from this nation. There is no guarantee against poverty equal to a job for every man.[1]

—Herbert Hoover

When Herbert Hoover spoke those words in 1928, shortly before he was elected the thirty-first president of United States, many American citizens had good reason to believe his optimistic prediction. The nation was enjoying one of the most prosperous periods in its history, and commentators had begun referring to it with upbeat nicknames like the New Era and the Roaring Twenties.

The economy had been in a state of explosive, soaring growth since the early 1920s, and numerous Americans, from business executives to laborers, had benefited from the upswing. Driven by new technological innovations, the productivity of U.S. industries had nearly doubled, and household wages and buying power were higher than ever before. As a result, a growing number of people were able to purchase homes and acquire appliances, radios, automobiles, and other goods that had been unattainable luxuries a few years earlier. As such items became more commonplace in American homes and driveways, they provided powerful symbols of the nation's affluence. Consumer purchasing also played an important role in sustaining the boom, as companies built new factories, hired new workers, and churned out new products to meet rising demand. At the same time, the stock market seemed to be headed ever upward. The Dow Jones Industrial Average nearly doubled in value between 1927 and 1929, giving

Economic prosperity in the 1920s took many forms, including soaring rates of automobile ownership.

investors of all stripes the hope that they could quickly reap profits by putting money into stocks.

Perhaps most importantly for middle-class and working-class Americans, the booming economy created jobs. The nation's unemployment rate—the percentage of the civilian work force seeking jobs but unable to find employment—averaged just over 3 percent between 1925 and 1929, lower than in any other five-year period in the previous three decades.[2] With optimism and affluence on the rise, Herbert Hoover's talk of a job for every person who wanted one seemed well within reach.

Within the span of a few years, however, the hope of full employment was completely shattered. Instead, the United States was rocked by the most severe economic collapse and the highest rate of joblessness in its history. The Great Depression, which began in the fall of 1929 and continued for more than a decade, grew into such an epic crisis that it cast doubt upon many of the essential convictions that Americans had held about their country. Foremost among these was the belief that the United States was a land of ever-expanding opportunities, where ability and hard work would be rewarded. Moreover, with millions of people thrown out of work, the Great Depression forced the nation to reassess its unsympathetic attitude toward those who were unemployed and to consider bold new methods of assisting those who had been plunged into poverty.

The Crash and Its Victims

The Great Depression began with a shocking stock market crash in 1929. Between October 21 and 29 of that year, stock prices on the New York Stock Exchange went into a sudden and severe nosedive. The biggest sell-off occurred on "Black Tuesday," October 29. Stock values continued to spiral downward in the weeks that followed. By mid-November the market had lost almost half of its value from two months earlier, when prices had peaked. This startling drop translated into countless stories of misery for the individuals and businesses that had invested heavily in the market. People who had been millionaires according to their stock portfolios became destitute in a matter of days. The crash was equally brutal on smaller investors, wiping out the life savings of countless people.

Although the causes of the 1929 crash were complex and are still subject to debate, at the root of the matter was a simple truth: massive investments of money into the market in the years before the crash had caused the prices of most stocks to soar far above their true values. This created a so-called "bubble" in stock values, and when that bubble burst, prices plummeted. Most overvaluations of this kind do not lead to such an extreme and widespread free-fall in prices. The massive sell-off of 1929, then, was more than a simple price correction. It also reflected and exposed deep problems with America's economic foundations.

One factor was that several important business sectors—farming, textile manufacturing, mining, and banking—had faced difficulties throughout the 1920s. These underperforming industries ultimately created a drag on the economy as a whole. Another issue was that the prosperity of the New Era was felt more strongly in some locations than others. While the large urban cities of the East and West Coasts and the Midwest had enjoyed strong growth during the 1920s, rural regions (of the South and Midwest in particular) had languished.

In addition, the mass consumer buying that had become a centerpiece of the economy had its limits. Even at the peak of the economic upswing in the late 1920s, less than 30 percent of American families had the financial resources

A crowd of people gather outside the New York Stock Exchange following the Crash of 1929.

to acquire homes, cars, and all the other comfortable symbols of middle-class existence. Overconfident industries thus ended up producing far more products than they could sell. Some of these same economic weaknesses also were present in other parts of the world. This limited the demand for American goods in other nations. All of these factors, combined with the widespread overvaluation of stocks, brought Wall Street crashing down—and prevented it from recovering before it sent the entire U.S. economy into a perilous tailspin.

Sliding into the Great Depression

The stock market crash produced an almost immediate downturn in demand for all kinds of products and services. This development forced businesses to cut back on their operations—which meant cutting their labor forces. By January 1930, less than three months after Black Tuesday, the national unemployment rate

A policeman stands guard outside the entrance to New York's closed World Exchange Bank, March 20, 1931.

had jumped from a pre-crash 3 percent to around 9 percent.[3] Despite some brief glimmers of hope that the economy might recover in the early months of 1930, the slide continued. The civilian work force unemployment rate for 1931 rose to 16.3 percent, and the following year that figure ballooned to 24.1 percent. By 1933—the peak year of Depression joblessness—nearly 13 million Americans were without jobs, and the unemployment rate reached a stunning 25.2 percent.[4] Some states and industrial cities suffered even higher rates of job losses. The state of Colorado, for example, reported that half of its workers were idled in 1932.

The unemployment statistics tell only part of the story, however, because many of those who managed to keep their jobs faced steep reductions in pay or hours. U.S. Steel, one of the titans of American industry, slashed wages by 10 percent in the fall of 1931, and by the following year many of its employees worked just two days a week. At that point, its operations had slowed to the point where it was turning out just 20 percent of the steel it was capable of producing. Numerous other businesses experienced similar slowdowns, resulting in frightening declines in every statistical measurement of economic activity in the United States. National income, gross national product, and manufacturing wages all declined by more than half in the initial years of the Depression.

The nation's tattered banking system also contributed to its worsening economic straits. Many of the nation's banks suffered huge losses in the stock market crash, both from their own investments and from risky loans made to stock speculators during the 1920s. When these financial problems became public knowledge, millions of Americans rushed to withdraw their money from banks and keep it at home. These so-called "bank runs" further damaged the health of banks. In 1930 more than 1,300 banks were unable to meet their obligations to customers and were forced to shut down. Although the bank closings initially affected mostly small institutions in small towns, in December 1930 the New York-based Bank of the United States closed. A wave of other large bank failures soon followed. By the end of 1931, another 2,300 banks had closed their doors.

These failures were catastrophic for millions of American families and business owners because bank deposits were not insured by the federal government at that time. Individuals and businesses simply lost whatever funds were in their accounts when the institution closed. The crisis also made those financial institutions that remained in business very cautious about lending money. As funding to finance new ventures dried up, economic activity continued to slow and jobs continued to evaporate.

The Face of Desperation

In the United States of the 1930s, unemployment benefits did not exist. People who lost their jobs thus found themselves in a very difficult situation. Most of the newly unemployed engaged in frantic searches for work, but with few jobs available and millions of people desperate to fill them, the odds of finding new work were extremely low. Throngs of applicants descended on the few companies that posted job openings, with scuffles sometimes breaking out among the job seekers.

Faced with almost-hopeless prospects, some job hunters abandoned their searches after a time. Others soldiered on, despite the terrible odds. One

Automobile for sale by an owner who, according to the sign, "must have cash" because he "lost all on the stock market."

woman described her unemployed husband as "always walking or looking. The places [he looks for work] are so far apart that his feet get sore. He's been everywhere—the day shifts and the night shifts. We had to put cotton in the heels of his shoes…. He's been back so often they hold up their hands when they see him coming."[5] Multitudes of people became so desperate for work that they left longtime communities or states of residence and migrated to other parts of the

"The Big Trouble"

In the following excerpt from *Boy and Girl Tramps of America*, a young man known only as "Texas" recounts how the hard times of the Depression affected his family and led to his life as a vagrant.

We got along swell before the big trouble came even if there were seven of us kids. I shined shoes in a barber shop. Jim carried papers. And Marie took care of Mrs. Rolph's kids. Mother always did some sewing for neighbors. We had a Chevvie and a radio and a piano. I even started to high school mornings, the year the big trouble came.

Dad got sick.... When he comes to go back to work he can't get a job, and everybody all of a sudden-like seems to be hard-up. I cut the price of shines to a nickel but it didn't help much. I even used to go around and collect shoes and ... shine and return them, but even then some weeks I couldn't make a dime.

Mrs. Rolph's husband got a [pay] cut and she cans Marie. Jim had to quit the paper route because he lost all his cash customers, and the others never paid. Nobody wanted mother to sew anything. And there we were, seven of us kids and Dad and Mother, and we couldn't make a cent....

country in fruitless quests for jobs (See "Chronicling the Difficulties of Depression-Era Unemployment," p. 161).

Not all families whose breadwinners lost their jobs faced immediate danger. Some unemployed men and women with savings or generous friends or family were able to evade the worst hardships. Many others, however, struggled for food, clothing, shoes, and other basic necessities. The evidence of that struggle became increasingly evident as the crisis intensified. Charity-sponsored soup kitchens sprang up in towns throughout the country to feed the growing number of people who could no longer put food on the table. Idled workers scrambled to collect a few coins by selling apples or "panhandling"—begging in public areas. In some cases, families were reduced to desperate foraging for food. "One woman went along the docks and picked up vegetables that fell from wag-

Oh, we tried hard enough, and everybody did their best. Marie made the swellest wax flowers. The kids peddled ironing cloths. Mother tried to sell some homemade bakery, and Dad did everything. We did our best, I guess, but it wasn't good enough....

All last winter we never had a fire except about once a day when Mother used to cook some mush or something. When the kids were cold they went to bed. I quit high school of course, but the kids kept going because it didn't cost anything and it was warm there.

In February I went to Fort Worth. Mother used to know a man there, and she thought maybe he could help me get a job. But he was as hard up as anybody else. I didn't want to return home and pick bread off the kids' plate so I tried to get work for a farmer for my board. Instead I got a ride to California. Near Salinas I worked in the lettuce fields, cutting and washing lettuce. I made $32 and I sent $10 home. But that was my first and last pay check. I got chased out of California in June....

Since then, ... I just been traveling.

Source

Minehan, Thomas. *Boy and Girl Tramps of America.* 1934. Reprint. Seattle: University of Washington Press, 1976, pp. 21-23.

ons," reported a social worker during a Senate hearing on unemployment. "On two different occasions the family was without food for a day and a half. Another family did not have food for two days. Then the husband went out and gathered dandelions and the family ate them."[6] In another Congressional hearing, a social worker described Philadelphia residents who "kept alive from day to day, catch-as-catch-can, reduced for actual subsistence to something of the status of a stray cat prowling for food."[7]

In many cases, the loss of employment meant the loss of a home as well. Legions of individuals and families faced eviction and foreclosure for not making their rent or mortgage payments. Between 1930 and 1932, some 600,000 people who had realized the dream of buying their own home saw that dream turn to dust as they were forced to give up their property. Evicted families stand-

Unemployed American workers wait in a San Francisco breadline.

ing forlornly on the sidewalk next to their piled belongings became another common scene of Depression despair.

Homelessness, in fact, became a national epidemic, with an estimated 2 million Americans lacking a permanent residence at the 1932-1933 peak of the Depression. They found shelter wherever they could. Some moved into abandoned buildings, some lived in tents and cars, and some erected crude shacks in makeshift camps that sprung up in parks, garbage dumps, and other open land in cities all across the country. The residents dubbed these communities "Hoovervilles"—a sarcastic tribute to President Herbert Hoover, who to many Americans symbolized a government that seemed unable or unwilling to help them.

President Hoover and the Conservative Response to the Depression

The president was certainly not oblivious to the economic and social miseries of the Depression and neither were members of Congress or other elected officials around the country. All had nervously watched the economy fall apart, and they faced mounting pressure to take action as conditions grew steadily worse. Nonetheless, there were relatively few efforts to mitigate the effects of the Depression on the national level until 1932—more than two years after the stock market crash.

The reasons for the slow response can be traced to several factors. First, many people expected the Depression to be relatively brief because earlier economic crises that had gripped the nation had given way to recovery within two or three years. In 1920-1921, for example, an economic recession had pushed the unemployment rate to nearly 12 percent. But that slowdown had lasted just a year and a half, and it had been followed by the robust growth of the New Era.

For Hoover and many other Republicans, the reluctance to take action also stemmed from their conservative approach to economic matters. The party had dominated national politics throughout the 1920s on the strength of *laissez faire* policies that minimized government intervention in business and economic affairs. Most Republicans believed that commerce should be controlled by the forces of the free market rather than by government regulation. Hoover summed up this philosophy in 1931 when he stated that "the sole function of government is to bring about a condition of affairs favorable to the beneficial development of private enterprise."[8]

The Republicans maintained this stance even after the Depression took hold of the nation. Party members believed that market forces inevitably would

President Herbert Hoover's conservative policies failed to spark an economic recovery.

get the economy back on track and that any forceful initiative on the part of government to accelerate this process would cause more harm than good. Many conservatives also opposed government intervention because they felt that it would be a dangerous step toward introducing elements of socialism and communism into the United States. Both of these political and economic philosophies called for much greater state control or ownership of national industries and natural resources. This fear had grown more pronounced since the 1922 establishment of the Communist-led Union of Soviet Socialist Republics (USSR) and the post-World War I outbreak of leftist revolutionary struggles in other part of the world.

Hoover held more moderate views on the role of government than some others in his party, so he did take some limited steps to respond to the crisis. In December 1929, for instance, he called together the heads of the nation's major industries and asked them—on a strictly volunteer basis—to avoid layoffs and to maintain wages at their present levels. Most of the business leaders agreed to the plan, although most of them eventually abandoned it when conditions failed to improve.

The president also pushed for increased spending on public works projects in order to get some unemployed Americans back to work. Hoover's use of public funds was very limited in comparison with the programs that would be enacted later in the Depression, but he hoped it would be sufficient to ease the nation's hardships until the economy got rolling again. The president also played a key role in the creation of the National Credit Corporation in 1931 and the Reconstruction Finance Corporation in 1932, both of which were intended to aid banks and other struggling businesses. Neither agency, however, proved effective in boosting the solvency of banks or encouraging new business investment.

On the whole, though, Hoover remained loyal to the conservative ideals of his party and argued that the federal government should maintain a largely hands-off approach to combating the Depression. This was especially true when it came to providing destitute citizens with some form of direct assistance—what was commonly referred to as "relief." The president was a strong believer in the ideal of rugged individualism, which he saw as the foundation of the nation's strength. He felt that the government should not take a strong role in offering assistance to its citizens because doing so would erode the freedom and independence of the individual and ultimately weaken the principles of hard work and personal initiative that had driven the country's progress. "You cannot extend the mastery of government over the daily lives of the people," the president said in regard to federal relief, "without at the same time making it the master of their souls and thoughts."[9]

Hoover and many other conservatives believed that any public assistance should come from local government—from cities, towns, and counties—rather than from state or federal government. In addition, Hoover encouraged charitable efforts to address the issues of joblessness, hunger, and poverty. To this end, he created the President's Emergency Committee for Employment and, later, the President's Organization for Unemployment Relief. Both groups focused on encouraging citizens to donate to charities; they provided no federal funding for relief.

The U.S. Relief System at the Dawn of the Depression

While many people perceived Hoover's attitude as hard-hearted, it was largely in keeping with the approach that American society had long followed with regard to poverty and unemployment. Ever since the colonial era, providing public assistance to the poor had been the responsibility of city or county government, and this locally based approach was still in place in the early years of the Great Depression.

In addition, Americans had always struggled with determining the appropriate level of assistance to extend to the poorest members of their communities. Generally, Americans had answered that question by dividing the destitute into two groups. Those who suffered hardship because of age or disability were seen as deserving of assistance. On the other hand, the so-called able-bodied poor—people who were physically able to provide for themselves but failed to do so—usually received minimal amounts of aid. These individuals were often perceived

This poster from New York's Emergency Unemployment Relief Committee urges financially secure Americans to make a charitable donation to less fortunate citizens.

as lazy and morally weak, and community leaders expressed concern that extending aid to them removed incentives for them to take care of themselves.

The U.S. relief system also depended heavily on private charities such as religious groups and immigrant-aid organizations to help the needy. As historian Walter I. Trattner notes, this trend became especially pronounced in the late 1800s, when "welfare work had become more of a private or voluntary matter than a public one."[10] Government agencies with public assistance functions became somewhat more prominent in the early 1900s, but private aid organizations were still very much on the front lines of social work at the time of the Depression. Their strong presence reflected the widespread belief that charitable giving, rather than government action, should be the primary vehicle for assisting the poor.

State-Level Efforts to Relieve Growing Misery

As months went by, however, the Depression completely overwhelmed the relief programs of local governments and private charities. Cities and counties quickly ran out of money, in part because the economic downturn reduced tax revenues that financed the assistance programs. Many local governments ran up huge deficits trying to meet their obligations, and most were simply unable to provide help for all who needed it. The resources of private groups were likewise depleted in short order. A comparison of conditions in Chicago between 1931 and 1932 makes clear the problems that the charities faced. In 1931, religious organizations and other aid groups extended some level of care to about half of the people in the city needing assistance. By the following year, the city's private aid groups could help less than 5 percent of the destitute.

When it became clear that local governments and private organizations did not have the resources to meet the needs of their suffering communities—and that the federal government was not prepared to intercede in any decisive way—state governments stepped in. Emergency aid agencies were established in most states during 1931 and 1932. Some states created agencies that were proactive and competently run, and they introduced financial assistance and relief programs that provided real help to struggling families. Others proved less willing or able to manage such an undertaking.

Moreover, all states faced difficulties in finding ways to pay for increased assistance. Many states did not assess income taxes in the early 1930s, and elected officials were very reluctant to increase other types of taxes at a time when so many people were facing financial difficulty. As the grim economic conditions persisted, even the states with the most effective and ambitious aid programs were overwhelmed by the scale of unemployment and poverty within their borders. These developments placed additional pressure on the federal government to get involved in the relief effort.

Unrest and the Fear of Revolution

As the country's economic foundation crumbled, Americans expressed growing fear that social order would dissolve as well. The majority of destitute citizens remained peaceful, but anger and discontent fueled an increasing number of tense and sometimes violent incidents. In January 1931, for example, hundreds of armed sharecroppers and tenant farmers in England, Arkansas, besieged a Red Cross office until they received food supplies. When a reporter asked the reason for their action, a woman responded that "our children are crying for food.... We are not going to let our children starve."[11] Riots and looting took place in other towns as well, with mobs ransacking stores for food and other goods.

Public demonstrations—often termed unemployment marches or hunger marches—were staged in cities all across the country and became particularly common during the spring and summer of 1931. The Communist Party USA, which touted itself as a champion of working men and women, was a driving force behind many of these events. The increased public profile of this group reflected the growing willingness of disillusioned Americans to consider political ideas and philosophies that they had dismissed as radical or unpatriotic only a few years.

Protests often provoked a strong response from city leaders, and police increasingly resorted to clubs and tear gas to break them up. One of the most infamous outbreaks of this sort of violence occurred in March 1932, during a protest at the Ford River Rouge Plant in Dearborn, Michigan. Local police and the company's private security force fired on the protestors with machine guns, leaving four people dead and more than sixty wounded.

The most infamous disturbance took place in Washington, D.C., in the summer of 1932. A group of military veterans known as the Bonus Expeditionary Force (BEF) encamped in the city for more than two months to demand immediate payment of a bonus that had been promised them for service in World War I. Though their protest was largely peaceful, it came to a violent end. U.S. Army troops led by General Douglas MacArthur used tanks, bayonets, and tear gas to drive the so-called Bonus Marchers out of the city. Federal officials

In July 1932 U.S. Army troops forcibly removed homeless veterans, known as Bonus Marchers, from Washington, D.C.

ordered such harsh action in part because they worried that the protestors might spark a wider revolutionary movement throughout the country.

The Turning Point: 1932

Against this backdrop of worsening social unrest and continued record rates of joblessness, conservative lawmakers felt increased pressure to extend some type of federal assistance. Congress thus passed three bills in the summer of 1932 that provided funds for work projects and other forms of relief. The bills then went to Hoover, who faced the decision of whether to sign the bills into law—thereby violating his oft-stated opposition to federal relief—or veto them and risk a severe public backlash. In the end, Hoover chose a middle course. He vetoed two of the bills, but he also signed the Emergency Relief and Con-

23

Democratic presidential nominee Franklin D. Roosevelt campaigning in Chicago in the summer of 1932.

struction Act of 1932. This legislation authorized $300 million for relief efforts, with the money to be loaned to states that had exhausted their own resources. This act marked the federal government's first involvement in assisting citizens suffering from unemployment and financial hardship. Though the expenditure was much smaller than those that would come later in the Depression, it provided a much-needed infusion of funds to the cash-starved states. By March 1933, these federal loans were underwriting 80 percent of the unemployment relief expenditures in the United States.

The year 1932 was also significant because it was a presidential election year. Hoover decided to seek another term in office, despite the fact that his popularity had been greatly weakened by the ongoing economic catastrophe. Among the Democrats, a number of candidates vied for the party's nomination. The ultimate victor in the Democratic primary was New York governor Franklin D. Roosevelt, often referred to as simply FDR (see Roosevelt biography, p. 145).

As the November election approached, voters had two distinct choices. President Hoover had been unable to revive the economy, and many middle- and working-class Americans viewed him as unresponsive to their needs and unmoved by their struggles. Moreover, he remained tied to the idea that the individual, not the government, would ultimately solve the problems of the Depression. His challenger offered a different approach. As governor, Roosevelt had strongly supported efforts to assist unemployed and impoverished citizens during the early years of the Depression. New York's Temporary Emergency Relief Administration was the first state agency to be established for this purpose, and it was viewed as one of the most effective aid offices in the country. Roosevelt promised similar action from the federal government if he was elected president, including an ambitious public works program to provide jobs.

During his campaign, Roosevelt hit upon several themes that struck a chord with the public. Focusing on the millions of unemployed whose lives had been devastated by the Depression, he spoke of the importance of the "forgotten man at the bottom of the economic pyramid."[12] He also pledged in his acceptance speech at the Democratic convention to introduce "a new deal" for the American people. Roosevelt's promises of bold action were warmly received—even when Roosevelt admitted that some of his efforts might not work. "The country needs, and unless I mistake its temper, the country demands bold, persistent experimentation," he declared. "It is common sense to take a method and try it. If it fails, admit it frankly and try another. But above all, try something."[13]

On November 8, the nation made its decision: Roosevelt was elected president by a margin of more than seven million votes, earning the support of 57 percent of the electorate. In addition, members of his Democratic Party won large majorities in both houses of Congress, which meant that the new president would have a great deal of legislative support for his programs and proposals. As 1933 dawned, the Roosevelt administration was about to have its opportunity to "try something," and the country waited anxiously to see what form his promised "new deal" would take.

Notes

[1] Quoted in Edsforth, Ronald. *The New Deal: America's Response to the Great Depression.* Malden, MA: Blackwell, 2000, p. 13.

[2] Lebergott, Stanley. *Manpower in Economic Growth: The American Record since 1800.* New York: McGraw-Hill, 1964, p. 512.

[3] Shlaes, Amity. *The Forgotten Man: A New History of the Great Depression.* New York: HarperCollins, 2007, p. 96.

[4] Lebergott, p. 512.

[5] Quoted in Watkins, T. H. *The Hungry Years: A Narrative History of the Great Depression in America.* New York: Holt, 1999, p. 57.

[6] Quoted in Trattner, Walter I. *From Poor Law to Welfare State: A History of Social Welfare in America.* 2nd ed. New York: Free Press, 1979, p. 224.

[7] Quoted in Brock, William R. *Welfare, Democracy, and the New Deal.* Cambridge, UK: Cambridge University Press, 1988, p. 163.

[8] Quoted in Taylor, Nick. *American Made: The Enduring Legacy of the WPA: When FDR Put the Nation to Work.* New York: Bantam, 2008, p. 8.

[9] Quoted in Trattner, p. 225.

[10] Trattner, p. 177.

[11] Quoted in Watkins, p. 109.

[12] Roosevelt, Franklin D. "The Forgotten Man, April 7, 1932." New Deal Network: Works of Franklin D. Roosevelt. Retrieved from http://newdeal.feri.org/speeches/1932c.htm.

[13] Quoted in DiNunzio, Mario R. *Franklin D. Roosevelt and the Third American Revolution.* Santa Barbara, CA: Praeger, 2011, p. 48.

Chapter Two

THE FIRST NEW DEAL WORK PROGRAMS

> Our greatest primary task is to put people to work. This is no unsolvable problem if we face it wisely and courageously. It can be accomplished in part by direct recruiting by the Government itself, treating the task as we would treat the emergency of a war.[1]

> —Franklin D. Roosevelt

O n March 4, 1933, Franklin Delano Roosevelt took the oath of office and became the thirty-second president of the United States. His inaugural address that day became a touchstone for many of the millions of people who heard it via radio. It offered them a new sense of hope that their government was going to take, in the president's words, "direct, vigorous action"[2] to combat the Great Depression. Roosevelt made good on this promise by initiating an ambitious set of economic programs in his first months in office. This early period of intense activity came to be known as Roosevelt's "100 Days," and Americans referred to Roosevelt's many different first-term economic initiatives as the New Deal.

Even after he implemented this early whirlwind of programs and initiatives, Roosevelt did not rest. He continued to take bold steps to attack the nation's high unemployment rate, and he ultimately went farther than any previous president in using the power of the federal government to address joblessness and poverty and influence the U.S. economy.

Roosevelt's efforts on the employment front were quite diverse, and they necessitated the creation of many different programs that were launched at different times. This wide-ranging approach reflected the president's willingness to experiment, but it also stemmed from other Depression-era factors, including the challenge of financing new government programs, the fast-changing political environment, the and president's own personal attitudes about relief programs.

The Works Progress Administration (WPA) proved to be the most expansive of the work and relief initiatives rolled out by the Roosevelt administration. But it was not established until 1935, two years into Roosevelt's presidency. The WPA was preceded by a number of other programs and agencies designed to get American workers and families back on their feet again.

The Dangers of "the Dole"

While Roosevelt could be innovative in some respects, he still had strong—and in some ways rather conservative—convictions about how best to assist Americans who had fallen on hard times. Like President Hoover, he strongly disliked the idea of "the dole"—directly giving money or goods to those in need without requiring the recipients to perform any type of work. The dole system—a reference to the government "doling out" benefits to citizens—had been implemented in several other countries, most notably Great Britain. Following World War I, that nation had instituted a national unemployment insurance program that made payments to those without jobs.

The dole, also termed "direct relief," faced a great deal of resistance in the United States. Many Americans believed that if public assistance was made too readily available, it would undermine the ideals of liberty and hard work that they held dear, while also weakening the moral fiber of individuals and of the nation as a whole. Roosevelt shared these misgivings. He believed that the crisis conditions he inherited required a certain amount of direct relief, but he was determined to build an economic recovery plan that did not depend heavily on such systems. The president and his administration thus turned to work relief.

Under this approach, the government funded projects that employed people to work rather than simply distributing money and goods to people without any conditions. Individuals hired in such programs were engaged in productive tasks that contributed to the public good. Supporters of such arrangements said that the programs not only allowed participants to avoid some of the stigma of taking a "government handout," they also helped them to maintain or develop work place skills. Moreover, administration officials predicted that work relief would "prime the pump" of the national economy by putting more money into circulation and creating more demand for materials, goods, and services.

Financing the New Deal

The new agencies and programs that were launched by the Roosevelt administration all cost money to operate. To cover the expense, the government needed to take money from other programs, raise taxes, or incur budget deficits—in other words, to borrow money. Ultimately, it both raised taxes and ran up a deficit. The administration's main tax increase, which targeted the nation's wealthiest citizens, did not take place until 1935. So-called deficit spending, on the other hand, began almost immediately. For the fiscal years 1934 through 1937, the budget shortfall totaled nearly $18 billion, which up to that point was more debt than the government had ever taken on except during times of war. Although President Roosevelt did not like the prospect of incurring deficits, he thought the severity of the crisis facing America gave him no choice.

Work relief was by no means a new idea. It had been employed on a limited basis by city governments during previous recessions and by state relief agencies in 1931 and 1932. The federal government and individual states had also long used construction of so-called public works—roads, bridges, schools, canals, and other infrastructure used by the general public—to create jobs and boost economies. Under Roosevelt's New Deal, however, the federal government embraced these programs and projects on a scale never seen before. Some members of the Roosevelt administration so strongly believed in this approach that they sounded like religious missionaries when describing its advantages. "Give a man a dole and you save his body and destroy his spirit; give him a job and pay him an assured wage, and you save both body and spirit,"[3] proclaimed Harry Hopkins, who would ultimately head three different New Deal agencies involved with work relief (see Hopkins biography, p. 129).

There were drawbacks to such a system, however. Work relief programs were more complex, more time-consuming to manage, and more expensive than direct relief. These were important considerations for an administration that was intent on providing speedy assistance to desperate citizens. In addition, work-relief programs faced opposition from some private business interests who worried about competition from government-funded jobs initiatives. Business owners and executives also expressed concern that big work-relief programs could reduce the availability of low-cost labor. Labor unions expressed reservations as well, charging that if the pay rates for work-relief jobs were set at a low level, they could drive down wages for all workers. Finally, many people—especially upper-class Americans whose careers and financial security were not threatened by the Depression—opposed the concept of work relief. They viewed increased government involvement in economic endeavors as a violation of the principles of individualism and personal liberty. For some of these critics, Roosevelt's work-relief proposals represented a dangerous step toward a communist-style system in which all aspects of the economy would be planned and controlled by the state.

The Federal Emergency Relief Administration

Roosevelt's plans for restoring American jobs and reducing the economic misery of the Depression depended heavily on the talents of Hopkins, who had been directing assistance efforts for the State of New York since 1931. Hopkins

arrived in Washington in March 1933 with a detailed relief plan that became the blueprint for the Federal Emergency Relief Administration (FERA). He was appointed director of this new federal agency after Congress approved its funding in May.

The creation of FERA marked an important development in the provision of public assistance. Congress initially allocated a total of $500 million to the agency—$200 million more than had been approved the previous year in the Emergency Relief and Construction Act of 1932. Moreover, these funds were provided to the states not as loans that the states would eventually have to pay back, but as "matching-fund grants"—meaning that the federal government agreed to match on a dollar-for-dollar basis any funds that states set aside for relief pro-

Harry L. Hopkins led three New Deal work relief agencies, including the Federal Emergency Relief Administration (FERA).

grams. This approach meant that the federal government would shoulder a greater share of the cost for public assistance.

FERA did have to work closely with state governments, however, and this process did not always go smoothly. In several instances, Hopkins and his staff locked horns with state officials who refused to allocate funds for relief or who tried to use the dispersal of relief dollars to advance their political careers. Eventually, FERA took full control of relief operations in several uncooperative states.

Because of the need to dispense aid to many suffering people in a short amount of time, FERA put a lot of its resources into direct relief. But Hopkins also made work relief an important part of the agency's mission. FERA ultimately employed about two million people in jobs programs over its thirty-one-month existence, and it pioneered some of the methods that would later be adopted by the WPA.

One of the most important FERA innovations involved funding diverse types of employment. In addition to conventional public works projects such as roadbuilding, FERA financed programs to make clothing and bedding, and it hired tens of thousands of teachers to conduct classes, particularly in literacy and vocational subjects.

As FERA unfurled its various direct and work-relief efforts, agency officials confronted the essential question of how to determine whether people applying for relief were truly in need. Following the example previously set by most state and local officials, FERA adopted the practice of requiring applicants to undergo a means test, which meant closely scrutinizing people asking for aid to determine whether they qualified for help. "Every application has to be investigated," explained Hopkins in testimony before Congress. "We have to send investigators out to visit families, to look up the bank accounts, and look up insurance, and to see whether the relatives can take care of the applicants or not."[4]

Means testing helped prevent undeserving people from fraudulently claiming benefits, and the practice became a routine part of most of the New Deal assistance efforts during the Depression. Nonetheless, most relief recipients greatly resented the fact that caseworkers probed into the personal details of their lives, and they found the process very demeaning. "The interview was utterly ridiculous and mortifying," remembered one Depression-era relief applicant. "There were questions like: Who are your friends? Where have you been living? Where's your family? … Why should anybody give you money? … I came away feeling I didn't have any business living anymore. I was imposing on somebody."[5]

A FERA vocational training camp for unemployed women in Pennsylvania.

For many people, means testing added to the shame they felt at not being able to support themselves or their families. Their embarrassment tended to be more pronounced when they were granted direct relief, which was widely interpreted as a charitable handout. This attitude further underlined the appeal of work relief, which gave recipients the opportunity to earn the aid they received.

The Civilian Conservation Corps

At the same time that Hopkins and other New Deal leaders were drawing up plans for FERA, the Roosevelt administration launched another initiative that provided an even purer expression of work relief. In the first few weeks of Roosevelt's presidency, Congress passed legislation proposed by the White House to establish an agency that would use unemployed young men to combat soil erosion and other environmental problems afflicting the nation. On April 5, 1933, Roosevelt signed Executive Order 6101, which formally established the Civilian Conservation Corps (CCC). Within three months, 300,000 people had joined the corps.

According to Roosevelt, the CCC was intended to focus on "simple work, … confining itself to forestry, the prevention of soil erosion, flood control and similar projects."[6] The Roosevelt administration selected this mission for several reasons. First, outdoor-oriented projects on public lands were less likely to be perceived as a threat to private enterprise. Second, signs of severe soil erosion from poor farming practices were building across the Great Plains region of the United States (in the mid-1930s this problem would contribute to the phenomenon known as the Dust Bowl, in which drought and dust storms ravaged the populations of several prairie states). Finally, conservation was an area of personal interest for the president, who had spent many years replenishing the forest on his family's estate in Hyde Park, New York.

A poster encouraging young American males to sign up with the Civilian Conservation Corps.

The CCC brought these environmental restoration practices to poorly used lands across the nation. CCC work crews ultimately planted some three billion trees. They also undertook numerous other projects, including restoration of erosion-damaged farm lands, controlling forest fires, restoring historic battlefields, and constructing hiking trails, campgrounds, service buildings, and other facilities in national and state forests, parks, and other public lands.

In deciding who would be eligible for service, the CCC adopted an approach similar to the military. It limited admission to men between the ages of eighteen and twenty-five who met basic height, weight, and health requirements (including a stipulation that they have at least three "serviceable" teeth for chewing on both their upper and lower jaws). The U.S. War Department ran the camps where the workers resided, while the Department of Labor, the Interior Department,

CCC enrollees working on a hillside in Maryland.

and the Department of Agriculture handled other aspects of the program. Like soldiers, the young men who joined the CCC were required to leave home to complete their service. Most were stationed in remote wilderness areas, sometimes thousands of miles from where they had lived. In return for their labor, the average member received $30 a month—$25 of which had to be sent home to assist their families. Although the pay was low by the standards of the day, in the hard times of the Depression there was no shortage of people who were glad to accept it. The enrollees also received free meals and housing in the camps, and they were given the opportunity to take literacy, academic, and vocational classes in the evenings. The educational component provided a valuable service for many young men who had previously received little formal schooling. Ultimately, some 40,000 people learned to read while serving as members of the CCC.

Life in the corps was not for everyone, and as many as one out of five inductees ended up dropping out of the program. The CCC also had a mixed record in regard to the hiring and treatment of minorities. African Americans made up only about 7 percent of the total inductees, despite the fact that the program aimed for a goal of 10 percent black participation—roughly equal to the proportion of African Americans in the U.S. population at the time. The shortfall stemmed mostly from the extremely poor record of minority hiring in the South. Moreover, most camps, regardless of their location, were segregated by race.

Despite these flaws, the CCC proved to be one of the most popular of all the New Deal programs. It was widely appreciated for the quality of its conservation and construction work, as well as for the positive impact it had on its young members. "The CCC gave us discipline and a work ethic, taught us how to get along with others, and enabled us to help our families back home," recalled one corps member. "It was an experience that enriched my life."[7] The program continued until 1942, when it was terminated in the wake of the nation's entrance into World War II. Over its nine-year history, it provided employment to about 2.75 million men.

The Public Works Administration

The New Deal effort to put people to work advanced on another front with the establishment of the Public Works Administration (PWA) in June 1933. The agency was created with the passage of the National Industrial Recovery Act, a piece of broad-ranging legislation that was a centerpiece of Roosevelt's early efforts to reinvigorate the economy. As its name implied, the PWA focused on public-works projects, particularly large-scale construction initiatives to build dams, bridges, buildings, and transportation facilities like airports and rail depots. Although the expenditure of federal tax money for such purposes was nothing new, the amount of money and the scope of building greatly expanded under the PWA. Congress initially provided it with $3.3 billion to cover two years of work, and additional funding was extended to the agency until 1939, when it closed down. All told, the PWA spent an estimated $6 billion on various projects across the country.

The PWA took a somewhat different approach to work projects than other New Deal agencies. Rather than managing the construction effort directly, the PWA contracted with private companies who were responsible for the actual building—an approach that made sense given the complex technical nature of many of the initiatives it undertook. As a result, though, the PWA never functioned as a work-relief agency in the strict sense of the word. Most

Two construction workers atop the San Francisco-Oakland Bay Bridge, which the Public Works Administration completed in 1936.

of the people hired to work on its projects were not selected from the relief rolls and did not have to undergo means testing because they were not directly paid by the federal government.

Harold L. Ickes, who was also Roosevelt's secretary of the interior, served as director of the PWA. Proud of his "Honest Harold" nickname, Ickes gained a reputation as a stickler for details. He exhaustively reviewed all aspects of the projects that were considered and carried out by the PWA. His meticulous management of the agency allowed it to avoid actions that could be labeled as wasteful or corrupt. The drawback was that the PWA moved at an extremely slow pace, and as a result, it had a limited impact on reducing unemployment and reviving the economy. The number of people at work on the agency's initiatives never exceeded 500,000 at a time. This number was dwarfed by the lightning-fast hire-and-build pace of two other New Deal agencies, the Civil Works Administration and the WPA.

Despite its limitations in regard to employment, the PWA was responsible for some of the most impressive and enduring construction projects of the New Deal era. PWA projects included the Hoover, Grand Coulee, and Bonneville Dams; the Triborough Bridge in New York City; the San Francisco-Oakland Bay Bridge in California; Washington National Airport; and the Skyline Drive scenic route in Virginia. On a smaller scale, it built schools, hospitals, housing projects, courthouses and other government buildings, sewage systems, roadways, naval ships, and much more. In total, the agency carried out more than 34,000 projects (including construction of almost 7,500 schools), and nearly every county in the nation benefited from its efforts.

The PWA also posted an impressive record in the area of social justice. African Americans made up nearly a third of the administration's payroll, and it required its contractors to meet specified quotas in hiring minorities at a time when African Americans otherwise would have been shut out of the jobs. In addition, the PWA used $45 million of its funding to build institutions such as schools and hospitals that primarily benefited members of America's black communities.

The Tennessee Valley Authority

Athough the idea of building hydroelectric dams to harness the power of the Tennessee River had been circulating since the early years of the 1900s, the dams became a reality only after President Roosevelt convinced Congress to establish the Tennessee Valley Authority (TVA) in May 1933. This ambitious project would ultimately transform a large section of the southeastern United States by bringing electricity and development to one of the poorest regions of the country.

The Roosevelt administration did not conceive the TVA primarily as a jobs program. However, the agency needed workers to construct its hydroelectric dams and related infrastructure, and huge numbers of job seekers turned up in the Southern communities where hiring took place. Those who were lucky enough to receive a job with the authority enjoyed relatively high pay. Unskilled

Tennessee Valley Authority (TVA) workers at Fort Loudon Dam, a hydroelectric dam in Tennessee.

laborers received 45 cents an hour for a 33-hour work week, which was roughly double the amount paid by the CCC.

Within three years of the TVA's creation, it had 13,000 people on its payroll, and construction work on various dams and other facilities continued through the early 1940s. While the number of jobs created did not equal the totals racked up by many of the other New Deal agencies, the TVA was a very valuable source of employment in a region that was especially hard hit by the Depression.

The Civil Works Administration

By the fall of 1933, FERA, CCC, TVA, and PWA were all providing jobs for desperate Americans. Nonetheless, the national unemployment numbers remained very high. Economists also forecast that unemployment rates would increase during the coming winter, as farm labor and other seasonal work dried up. This raised the possibility that FERA, even with its increased funding, would be unable to cope with the larger number of people who might be seeking relief. FERA director Harry Hopkins pondered the problem, came up with a plan of action, and presented his idea to Roosevelt on November 2. Hopkins wanted to create a crash program that would put four million people to work through the spring of 1934. It was a bold move, unlike any that had been attempted before, but the president was willing to give it a try. Roosevelt took $400 million from other New Deal programs to finance the effort, and on November 9 the Civil Works Administration (CWA) was created by executive order.

The CWA was a strictly federal operation, which freed it from the problems of dealing with state governments. This orientation, however, made CWA staffers responsible for managing everything from creating engineering plans for construction projects to establishing and managing an employment service to hire workers. Hopkins and his staff threw themselves at these tasks with feverish intensity, rushing to meet the hiring goals they had set. Within two weeks, 800,000 people were at work, and paychecks totaling nearly $8 million were being distributed at CWA offices around the country. By January 1934, the CWA had surpassed Hopkins's goal of employing four million Americans.

Those who received jobs with the CWA appreciated the work—as well as the fact that the agency was much less restrictive in regards to pay and hiring than the CCC and FERA. The CWA tended to offer wages that were in line with the minimum pay offered in private-sector jobs in the local community, and applicants were not required to undergo a means test. The only requirement for eligibility was that an individual be unemployed.

These relaxed hiring guidelines provoked complaints from some observers.

Workers with the Civil Works Administration (CWA) on a water main project in Minnesota.

They argued that CWA jobs should only go to the most needy, and that pay rates should be lower so that workers would have incentive to move back to private-sector jobs when they became available. Critics of the program also charged that CWA projects were "make work" assignments that accomplished little of use. There were oft-told stories about CWA workers engaging in useless tasks such as raking parks that had already been raked. While many of these tales were exaggerated, some CWA projects did suffer from poor planning in the rush to put millions of people to work.

Despite these shortcomings, the agency accomplished a great deal in a short amount of time. With 90 percent of the agency's funds directed to construction, CWA workers built or improved some 40,000 schools and constructed nearly 500 airports. Other common projects included building and repairing roads and bridges, renovating public buildings, and creating and improving parks. For the most part, these were small-scale projects that could be launched quickly and required a minimum amount of planning. In some instances, the agency took an imaginative approach in deciding what kinds of work could be funded, which allowed artists, archeologists, teachers, and researchers to participate.

The CWA proved popular with many members of the public. This popularity helped convince Congress to allocate additional money to the program in February 1934, after the original funding ran out. Some supporters hoped that the CWA would be extended indefinitely, but Roosevelt was unwilling to take that step. The president worried that a long-term program would worsen the budget deficit, and he feared that continued Republican criticism of the CWA would cause problems for Democratic candidates in the 1934 elections. The agency's operations came to an end in March 1934, a little less than five months after it started, and the effort ended up costing about $1 billion in total. Though short-lived, the CWA provided work and income to millions of people at a particularly difficult time of the Depression. It showed that the federal government was capable of quickly mobilizing a large-scale work relief effort, and it demonstrated that there was significant public support for such measures. Conversely, the loud, if somewhat limited, political opposition to the CWA made it clear that any expansive jobs program mounted by the federal government was going to be a source of controversy.

Much Accomplished, Much to Do

Within eight months of Roosevelt's inauguration, his administration had established five new federal agencies to place people in government-funded jobs. According to data from the Bureau of Labor Statistics, the workers hired in all of the nation's jobs programs reduced the unemployment rate by 4 percent in 1933 and 6 percent in 1934. The economic activity created by work relief programs may have sparked some additional hiring in the private sector as well. Beyond the numbers, the jobs programs helped improve national morale—no small feat given the dismal conditions that existed when Roosevelt took office.

The November 1934 midterm elections provided a clear indication that Roosevelt's approach to the Depression was winning favor with the majority of U.S. citizens. Although the president himself was not on the ballot, his policies dominated the campaigns for hundreds of seats in the U.S. Congress. Democratic candidates promised to support Roosevelt's New Deal. Meanwhile, Republicans warned that Congress needed to check the president's power to prevent him from establishing what the Republican national chair described as the "domination of an all-powerful central government."[8] When the votes were tallied, the Democrats made significant gains in both houses of Congress, guaranteeing the president widespread congressional support in the new year.

Roosevelt, his advisors, and the men and women managing the administration's various New Deal programs and agencies found this public validation of their efforts to be greatly encouraging. Nonetheless, the architects and managers of the New Deal also recognized that some 11.3 million Americans were still unemployed in 1934—more than 21 percent of the total working population. Moreover, the administration's efforts to revive the economy had not yet come anywhere close to restoring the prosperity that existed before the 1929 crash. The Great Depression was a long way from being over.

Notes

[1] Roosevelt, Franklin D. *The Public Papers and Addresses of Franklin D. Roosevelt,* Vol. 2. New York: Random House, 1938, p. 13.

[2] Roosevelt, p. 15.

[3] Quoted in Hopkins, June. *Harry Hopkins: Sudden Hero, Brash Reformer.* New York: St. Martin's, 1999, p. 164.

[4] Quoted in Brock, William R. *Welfare, Democracy, and the New Deal.* Cambridge, UK: Cambridge University Press, 1988, p. 186.

[5] Quoted in Terkel, Studs. *Hard Times: An Oral History of the Great Depression.* New York: Pantheon, 1986, p. 422.

[6] Roosevelt, p. 80.

[7] Quoted in Mulvey, Deb, ed. *We Had Everything but Money.* Greendale, WI: Reiman, 1992, p. 59.

[8] Quoted in Bondi, Victor, ed. *American Decades 1930-1939.* Detroit, MI: Gale, 1995, p. 238.

Chapter Three

FORMATION OF THE WORKS PROGRESS ADMINISTRATION

There may be a few things about any big program that we don't like. No matter how hard we try on any big job, something unexpected turns up. The only people who don't make mistakes are those who do nothing at all. The WPA is a great national enterprise to get something done. Mistakes may be made, but we can be sure the American people will not make the mistake of doing nothing.[1]

—WPA worker's handbook

In the wake of Democratic gains in the 1934 elections, the Roosevelt administration prepared new legislation to present to Congress. Roosevelt and his advisors realized that fellow Democrats in Congress had the power to enact additional far-reaching reforms and programs desired by the administration. "Boys, this is our hour," said Hopkins to his staff. "We've got to get everything we want.... Get your minds to work on developing a complete ticket to provide security for all the folks of this country up and down and across the board."[2]

Roosevelt unveiled a second round of economic reforms and programs in his annual message to Congress on January 4, 1935. This phase of the Roosevelt presidency, in fact, came to be known by contemporary observers and subsequent generations of historians as the "Second New Deal." The initiatives launched during this period included the establishment of the Social Security system and significant reforms affecting labor relations, banking, and taxation. The biggest program designed to address unemployment, however, was Roosevelt's most expansive and ambitious work-relief program yet: the Works Progress Administration (WPA).

Shifting Political Winds

Although Roosevelt's Second New Deal reflected the presence of a larger Democratic majority in Congress, there were other factors at play as well. By 1934, the political atmosphere in the United States had grown extremely tense and divisive. When he first took office, Roosevelt had tried to create a sense of national political unity to fight the Depression. That approach, however, had been battered by relentless conservative attacks on the New Deal. The president's adversaries—conservative Democrats in addition to Republicans—argued that Roosevelt's relief programs and other reform measures were endangering the nation's fiscal health, destroying traditional values, and threatening personal liberty. The more extreme critics even charged that Roosevelt was a radical who was intent on leading the nation toward communism.

Opponents also expressed alarm that New Deal programs were increasing the power of the federal government and reducing the autonomy of the states. States' rights were of particular concern to white Southerners who feared that federal officials would work to end the region's strict system of racial segregation. Powerful members of the business community had also resisted the New Deal's reform efforts, which further damaged the president's attempt to foster a cooperative approach to addressing the nation's problems.

At the same time, however, the Roosevelt administration felt extraordinary pressure to provide greater security and better living conditions for people from all walks of life. Some of this pressure came from within; Roosevelt and top officials in his administration recognized that millions of Americans still were suffering, and they wanted to help. But pressure also came from outside. By late 1934, some influential journalists and economists who supported the president and the New Deal were counseling Roosevelt to take even stronger steps (see "Walter Lippmann Urges a New Approach to Work Relief," p. 171). Around this same time, Roosevelt found himself in the crosshairs of several national economic reform and social justice movements headed by charismatic leaders.

Rising Tides of Social and Economic Activism

Three of these campaigns became particularly prominent. The National Union for Social Justice was founded in 1934 by Charles E. Coughlin, an influential Catholic "radio priest" based in the Detroit area. Coughlin had supported Roosevelt's early initiatives, but by 1934 he had decided that the president's allegiances lay with banks and big business, not the struggling poor. The priest

A political cartoon attacks Roosevelt's "New Deal Pump" as a horrible waste of taxpayer dollars.

began openly criticizing Roosevelt, and the National Union for Social Justice even put forth its own presidential candidate in the 1936 election. Coughlin also harbored strong anti-Jewish beliefs that became more evident by the close of the decade. In the late 1930s, in fact, his reputation became increasingly cloud-ed by his hateful attacks on Jews, who he blamed for the nation's banking woes. He also expressed steadfast opposition to U.S. involvement in the affairs of Europe even after the menacing rise of Adolf Hitler and Nazi Germany. Cough-

Catholic priest Charles Coughlin emerged during the mid-1930s as one of Roosevelt's harshest critics.

lin's influence waned dramatically in the early 1940s, after he made the ridiculous claim that America's entrance into World War II against Germany and Japan had been engineered by Jewish plotters.

Another influential social activist of the 1930s was Dr. Francis Townsend of Long Beach, California. In the early 1930s he became a forceful spokesperson for the elderly, many of whom were especially vulnerable to economic misfortune during the Depression. Townsend hatched a plan that called for the government to provide all citizens over age sixty-five with a monthly pension payment of $200. In return, the recipients would promise to retire (thus opening up jobs for younger people) and spend the pension payments (to stimulate economic activity). The so-called Townsend Plan never got far in Congress, but millions of older Americans became supporters of the proposal. Townsend's pension crusade, in fact, has been credited as a factor in the 1935 introduction of the U.S. Social Security system, which provides monthly financial assistance to senior citizens.

A more serious threat to Roosevelt's leadership came from Democratic senator Huey Long of Louisiana. Long instituted a range of progressive policies as governor of his home state during the 1920s. In the mid-1930s he launched a national Share Our Wealth movement that demanded an extreme redistribution of money from rich to poor. Under Long's plans, strict limits would be placed on personal income and family fortunes, with the excess reallocated through taxes to provide a guaranteed standard of living to all citizens. Long's efforts were particularly worrisome to Roosevelt because the senator made no secret of his desire to be president. He was widely expected to challenge Roosevelt for the Democratic nomination in 1936, and some observers thought he might threaten the president's re-election by running as a third-party candidate.

All of these forces combined to make Roosevelt reconsider his policies. Understanding that he could expect almost no backing from conservatives and

The Kingfish

One of the most polarizing figures of the Depression era, Huey Long had served in Louisiana state government since the 1910s and was elected governor in 1928. In the years that followed, he established a powerful political machine that made him the undisputed ruler of his state. In 1930 he even engineered his election to the U.S. Senate while retaining his position as governor (in 1932 Long turned over the governorship to a handpicked successor, but everyone recognized that he still controlled Louisiana).

The power of the man they called "the Kingfish" was rooted in his success as a "populist"—a champion of poor and middle-class citizens against selfish wealthy elites. This philosophy was especially appealing during the Depression. Long's supporters saw him as a defender of the downtrodden who wanted to ease the disparities between "the haves and the have-nots." Others viewed him as a dictator along the lines of fascist rulers such as Benito Mussolini of Italy—a dangerous demagogue who subverted the democratic system in his desire for power. Had he made good on his promise to run for president, that debate would have played out at the pinnacle of American politics. On September 8, 1935, however, Long was gunned down in the Louisiana capitol building by the son of a political rival. He died two days later.

Source

Hair, William Ivy. *The Kingfish and His Realm: The Life and Times of Huey P. Long.* Baton Rouge: Louisiana State University Press, 1996.

observing that strong support existed for social justice issues, he decided to move to the political left.

A New Agency Takes Shape

The Second New Deal reflected Roosevelt's strategic shift. He quickly pushed to install bold new government programs such as Social Security as permanent fixtures. This federal program, which was established with the passage of the 1935 Social Security Act, provided a source of guaranteed income for retirees and limited unemployment insurance for those who lost their jobs.

In addition to these permanent expansions of the federal "safety net" for economically vulnerable Americans, the Roosevelt administration launched another wave of ambitious measures to combat the effects of the Depression. The Works Progress Administration (WPA) was the centerpiece of this campaign to get at least 3.5 million unemployed Americans back to work. The administration envisioned the WPA as a longer-term version of the Civil Works Administration (CWA), which had existed for about five months in late 1933 and early 1934.

While the massive hiring proposed by Roosevelt was new, the president's philosophy regarding relief assistance remained the same. In creating the WPA, he wanted to end all types of "dole" direct assistance from the federal government. Once the WPA was up and running, the president planned to eliminate the Federal Emergency Relief Administration (FERA) and return responsibility for direct relief to state and local governments.

The Roosevelt White House drafted a bill allocating funding for the WPA and several other work programs and sent it to Congress for approval just two weeks after the president's January 1935 speech. It was notably short on specifics. The bill simply authorized the use of nearly $4.9 billion for the purpose of work relief, with all decisions about the money's allocation left to the president's discretion. That was an exceptionally large government appropriation in 1935, and it triggered criticism from observers who charged that it granted Roosevelt too much power. The House of Representatives nonetheless passed the measure in a matter of days, but the Senate balked at giving Roosevelt such a free hand. Over the next two months, conservative senators succeeding in adding provisions that more clearly defined how Roosevelt's WPA would operate. One revision, for example, required that wages for WPA jobs be set below the minimum pay that prevailed in each local area. This "security

Roosevelt, seen here before a 1934 radio address to the nation, pushed tirelessly for passage of the Emergency Relief Appropriation Act, which created the WPA.

wage" was intended to encourage Americans with WPA-relief jobs to keep pursuing higher-paying private-sector employment.

The amended bill—called the Emergency Relief Appropriation Act of 1935—was approved by both houses of Congress, and Roosevelt signed it into law on April 8. At that point, the president still had not decided who would run the expanded jobs program. The two leading contenders were the men who had overseen the largest work relief initiatives of the First New Deal, Harry Hopkins of FERA and CWA and Harold Ickes of the Public Works Administration (PWA). Both wanted the job, adding fuel to a heated rivalry that had grown between the two administrators over the previous years. In the end, Roosevelt was swayed by Hopkins's achievements with the CWA and his no-nonsense approach to his work.

"Harry gets things done,"[3] Roosevelt bluntly told a member of his administration. The president tried to soothe Ickes's feelings by assuring him he would have a voice in selecting the work-relief projects the WPA would undertake.

Building the WPA

On May 6, 1935, the president issued an executive order officially creating the Works Progress Administration. As Hopkins took the reins of the new agency, he borrowed liberally from other New Deal agencies he had led. The new agency's staff and its general organizational structure came directly from FERA, which was shut down to make way for WPA. In fact, FERA administrators and other employees at the federal, state, and local levels all began working for the WPA as soon as they wrapped up their FERA responsibilities.

As he had done with FERA, Hopkins created a lean agency that valued speedy decisions and used relatively little of its funding for staff salaries and office operations. Administrative costs made up just 4 percent of its spending during its first five years of operation—meaning that the vast majority of its money went toward paying workers and completing projects.

Roosevelt outlined his goals for the agency in a radio broadcast on April 28, 1935. During this evening address, the president assured listeners across the country that the WPA projects "shall be of a nature that a considerable proportion of the money spent will go into wages for labor."[4] To this end, WPA emphasized straightforward projects such as road construction and park renovation because they used a lot of manual labor, did not require extensive amounts of specialized materials or design work, and could be launched in almost any community (see "President Roosevelt Discusses the Works Progress Administration," p. 174).

This emphasis on identifying labor-intensive projects that could be launched quickly—"shovel-ready" projects, in the words of WPA officials—made a huge impact. The Works Progress Administration quickly became the most important of all the New Deal work-relief programs. In the three-year period between 1935 and 1938, in fact, the agency accounted for about three-fourths of all federal work-relief employment in the United States.

Managing the WPA

In deciding how work projects would be managed, Hopkins followed the approach that had been pioneered with the CWA: the WPA assumed direct con-

WPA enrollees working on a street project in Detroit, Michigan.

trol, making all the hiring decisions itself rather than contracting with outside companies. Moreover, the WPA was a wholly federal operation, meaning that it could avoid some bureaucratic wrangling with state government officials.

Still, WPA projects required cooperation and input from a diverse cast of characters. WPA officials decided it was impractical for them to come up with local projects themselves. Instead, they asked groups that had more familiarity with local needs to submit project proposals. These groups—referred to as sponsors—were usually city or county governments, but state governments, other federal agencies, and assorted other public entities could propose ideas as well.

Sponsoring groups were expected to take on a share of the total cost of approved WPA projects. For the first four years that the WPA was in operation, the average ratio was 80/20: the federal government covered about 80 percent of the cost of each project by writing the paychecks for the workers, while the sponsoring group paid the remaining 20 percent by picking up the cost of materials, tools, and other necessary services. This formula was flexible, however, depending on the project and resources available to the sponsor, so the WPA sometimes assumed a larger share of the cost. In 1939 Congress instituted tighter control of this aspect of WPA operations by requiring the sponsoring group to pay 25 percent of the bill. Even after that change, however, the WPA's funding of work projects was relatively generous. As a result, the agency took on more projects than the PWA. The latter agency required local and state governments to contribute as much as 55 percent of the cost of the construction projects they requested. Many sponsors could not or would not pay that percentage, so they turned to the WPA.

The WPA also followed the example of the CWA in creating a large number of relatively small work projects (many costing less than $25,000) that could put a lot of people to work in short order. This emphasis on small projects distinguished WPA from PWA, which devoted its energy to dams, bridges, and other massive public works projects. The WPA's approach employed more people per dollar spent than the PWA because less of its funding had to be diverted to engineering, equipment, and materials. Still, the WPA did become involved in larger efforts at times, including the construction of large airports and office buildings, and even entire towns.

Boondoggle Fears

Local governments were quick to take advantage of the arrival of the WPA. They began sending ideas for public work projects into the Washington headquarters of the WPA almost as soon as the agency was created. If these proposals passed an initial review, they were passed to the Advisory Committee on Allotments, a group that included representatives from the WPA, other federal agencies, and business and labor organizations. If the advisory committee signed off on the project, it went to President Roosevelt for final approval.

This multi-level system reflected the care that the Roosevelt administration took in rolling out and managing its New Deal work-relief programs. Roosevelt, Hopkins, and other officials wanted to fight the widespread perception that government-created employment projects were wasteful exercises in busy work. This charge had been lobbed at all of the New Deal work-relief programs, and reports of frivolous endeavors were often played up in the press—particularly by conservative newspapers that opposed Roosevelt's policies. Critics even coined a new term—"boondoggle"—to describe misguided government-sponsored tasks that had little value. (The word originally referred to simple craft activities taught in an FERA class, but critics of New Deal work programs seized it for their own use.)

Roosevelt confronted this issue head-on when he announced the WPA initiative in January 1935. Item number one among his "practical principles" for the program was that "all work undertaken should be useful—not just for a day, or a year, but useful in the sense that it affords permanent improvement in living conditions or that it creates future wealth for the nation." This directive was fresh in everyone's mind in the spring and summer of 1935, as the Advisory Committee on Allotments dug through piles of work proposals and the WPA staff worked to get the agency up and running.

Some observers worried that the president's demand for "useful" work might cause WPA decision makers to be overly cautious in approving projects. Hopkins and other agency administrators, however, knew that their overriding mission was to put millions of Americans back to work, so they considered proposals with an open mind and a flexible approach to what might be useful (see "Hallie Flanagan Describes Harry Hopkins's Ideas about Work Relief," p. 183).

As a result, the projects carried out by the WPA during the Great Depression encompassed an extremely wide range of tasks and involved everyone from laborers armed with shovels and pickaxes to artists wielding paintbrushes and musical instruments. "Never forget," Hopkins reminded his administrators, "that the objective of this whole project is … taking 3,500,000 off relief and putting them to work, and the secondary objective is to put them to work on the best possible projects we can, but we don't want to forget that first objective."[6]

Notes

[1] *Our Job with the WPA*. Washington, DC: U.S. Government Printing Office, n.d., p. 21.
[2] Lawson, Alan. *A Commonwealth of Hope: The New Deal Response to Crisis*. Baltimore, MD: Johns Hopkins University Press, 2006, p. 120.
[3] Quoted in Taylor, Nick. *American Made: The Enduring Legacy of the WPA: When FDR Put the Nation to Work*. New York: Bantam, 2008, p. 170.
[4] Roosevelt, Franklin D. *The Public Papers and Addresses of Franklin D. Roosevelt*, Vol. 4. New York: Random House, 1938, p. 135.
[5] Roosevelt, p. 21.
[6] Quoted in McKinzie, Richard D. *The New Deal for Artists*. Princeton, NJ: Princeton University Press, 1973, p. 80.

Chapter Four

WPA
CONSTRUCTION PROJECTS

⊷ⷛⷊⷜⷜⷛⷛ

My husband and daughter were employed by the WPA....
Without the little money they brought in, we wouldn't have
been able to survive. Many times I thought that some days we
would have to go downtown to those soup lines, but with the
help of God, we never did.[1]

—A resident of East Texas recalling the Great Depression

For most of its employees, the Works Progress Administration meant work in the traditional sense of the word: basic manual labor to build something—a road, building, swimming pool, sidewalk, or some other piece of public infrastructure. Over the eight years of the agency's existence, three of every four of its employees were engaged in construction work of this kind.

But while most WPA building projects were straightforward in design, the logistics of mobilizing millions of workers to labor on thousands of different projects were enormously complex. Undaunted, WPA director Harry Hopkins and his staff quickly fashioned a system to handle hiring, payroll, training, and numerous other aspects of the agency's operations. By the fall of 1935, work was underway at numerous WPA construction sites, and the nation began to see the "dirt fly"[2]—a term Roosevelt had used in announcing the program. The workers who joined the WPA work force once more had a job, a sense of purpose, and a much-needed paycheck. Many of them, however, also discovered that working for the WPA—like working for virtually any company or government agency—brought its share of frustrations and problems.

WPA Hiring Practices

When Roosevelt explained the principles of the WPA to the nation in his radio broadcast of April 28, 1935, he stated that the agency's projects "must be of a character to give employment to those on the relief rolls."[3] In other words, the president wanted to use the agency to move people from direct relief to work relief. He made this a point of policy when he issued an executive order that required each WPA project to hire at least 90 percent of its employees from the relief rolls, except in special circumstances. That ratio jumped to 95 percent in 1937. The administration decided that it was impractical to hire 100 percent of WPA workers from direct relief rolls, however, because even small construction projects usually required some workers with specialized skills—and such workers generally were able to keep busy enough to avoid direct relief programs.

The WPA emphasis on hiring people enrolled in direct relief programs helped insure that the jobs would be awarded to the genuinely needy, since direct relief recipients underwent a means test when they applied for assistance (see "The WPA Explains Its Mission," p. 187). This rule also favored individuals who had been unemployed for a long period, because they likely already received direct relief and thus qualified for WPA work. The drawback to this policy—at least in the minds of many job seekers—was that it forced people who hoped to obtain WPA work to first apply for direct relief, if they had not already done so. This step forced many Americans to endure the humiliation of applying for public assistance—a process that included submitting to widely despised means testing.

The WPA initially limited employment to those age sixteen and older, but the minimum age was raised to eighteen in 1938. Relatively few jobs went to the youngest eligible applicants, however, because the WPA gave preference to individuals who had a family to provide for. Those people naturally tended to be older adults. Moreover, job seekers who had reached middle age often had a more difficult time finding work in the private sector, so they tended to remain in direct relief programs for longer periods. Throughout the history of the agency, at least one-third of its work force was age forty-five and above.

The WPA also limited employment to one person per household in order to spread the benefits of work relief as widely as possible. Exceptions were occasionally made to the one-job-per-family rule, but they were rare. In deciding which adult family member would be hired, the WPA gave preference to the head of the household—the person who had traditionally been the wage earn-

WPA employees at a New Jersey glassmaking factory.

er, which in most cases was the father. This was part of the reason that the great majority of WPA workers were men.

Pay and Hours on WPA Projects

Employees of the WPA did not get rich on the paychecks they received. To the contrary, WPA jobs paid less than comparable positions in private industry because of the security wage requirements that had been added to the Emergency Relief Appropriation Act of 1935. The size of employee paychecks depended on several factors, including the area of the country in which the person worked and the level of skill required for each job. Unskilled laborers earned from $19 to $44 a month (about $320 to $740 in 2012 dollars), while skilled workers were paid $55 to $94 per month (about $925 to $1,580 in 2012 dollars). The unskilled workers struggled to get by on these payments, particularly if they had large families to support. In some cases the wages from a WPA job were even smaller than the meager amount a family had previously received through direct relief payments. In these situations, WPA workers could apply for supplementary relief payments to make up the difference.

WPA pay was also low because most employees worked less than the standard forty-hour work week that was becoming common in the 1930s. Initially, most WPA workers put in no more than 120 to 140 hours per month, the equivalent of about 28 to 32 hours per week. In 1936 the agency adopted a policy of paying an *hourly* rate that equaled the pay for similar jobs in the local area, but the total *monthly* amount a worker could take home still could not exceed their specified security wage. The practical effect of this policy was that employees worked fewer hours each month for the same amount of pay.

In 1939 the situation changed yet again, and the standard schedule for all WPA workers became 130 hours a month or 30 hours per week. On occasion, some employees did put in more hours than the totals noted above. Administrators, for example, sometimes permitted workers with important specialized skills to exceed the limits. Even then, however, WPA rules kept employees working under the forty-hour work week limitations. Temporary exceptions were granted only in extreme emergencies or when a project had fallen badly behind schedule due to severe weather events or other outside factors.

Because they worked fewer than forty hours a week, WPA employees were sometimes able to pick up temporary jobs on off days. "Moonlighting" in this manner could provide a much-needed boost to a family's income, but opportunities for extra work were limited given the poor state of the economy. On the other hand, WPA workers—and construction workers in particular—also faced the possibility of serious reductions in their hours. Cold, rain, and snow often brought building projects to a standstill, and WPA employees were not paid when they did not work. Repeated delays due to weather or other causes could leave a worker in perilous financial circumstances.

The WPA payroll system posed other problems for employees as well. The government usually distributed paychecks twice a month rather than weekly, and delays in distributing the checks were common. These distribution patterns posed a hardship to many financially strapped families who struggled to survive during these long payment gaps. A Georgia WPA worker voiced his unhappiness in a 1935 letter to President Roosevelt. "They have cut us down to 17-1/2 cent [an hour] and I can't make anything at that rate," he said. "They pay us every 2 weeks and then some time we don't have enough food to last."[4]

WPA construction workers engage in excavation for a new sewage plant in San Diego.

On the Job

Despite these misgivings and frustrations, however, most WPA workers expressed appreciation that they were gainfully employed and no longer dependent on direct relief payments (see Mr. Mahoney biography, p. 137). "[Direct] relief means charity. It means that one is taking something for nothing," explained one WPA laborer. "On WPA you work for what you get."[5]

For Americans employed on WPA construction projects, that work often involved strenuous labor. Some of the employees at WPA work sites were accustomed to these physically demanding tasks, but others were completely unfamiliar with blue-collar work. The demands of heavy construction work posed a challenge for these newcomers, especially for individuals who were middle-aged and older. "It was a shame to expect a white-collar person of 50 to dig sewers,"[6] complained the wife of one such employee.

Nonetheless, many of these individuals gamely threw themselves into their new vocation because they felt grateful for any type of employment (see "Residents of the Southern United States Recall the WPA," p. 179). One study of Depression-era work-relief programs related the experiences of a Mr. Klein, who worked on a WPA mosquito-control project in New York City:

> He came home covered with mud and oil, wearing heavy boots and looking like a laborer. At first Mrs. Klein was ashamed that the neighbors should see him looking like this. But he was happier working and so was she. There were times when his rheumatism bothered him so much that he did not see how he could continue. Despite this, he went on because it meant that he had a job.[7]

Combating the "We Piddle Around" Charge

The productivity of WPA employees was a topic of much debate throughout the history of the agency. Tales of workers taking a leisurely approach to their jobs were widely reported, and some Americans took to joking that the WPA initials stood for "We Piddle Around." Many of these anecdotes about lazy and unmotivated workers were sensationalized and exaggerated, however, and WPA officials claimed that they were usually spread by people who had no firsthand experience with the agency and who opposed the entire principle of work relief.

Accounts of the workers themselves indicate that conditions varied greatly between different WPA jobs. When projects were poorly planned and supervised, the work often proceeded slowly and inefficiently. In many cases, however, employees found the demands of the WPA workplace to be similar to what they had experienced with private employers. "When people talk about, you know, leaning on the shovel, well, we did a whole lot of work. And a whole lot of hard work," remembered a man who built roads with the WPA in North Carolina. "It wasn't no different than no other job. You earned the money."[8]

The impression that the agency employed loafers stemmed in part from other issues that were out of their control. First, the WPA was fundamentally different from private employers in that its primary goal was to put numerous people to work. This goal ran counter to the private-business ideal of getting the maximum amount of productivity out of the fewest number of employees. Not surprisingly, then, WPA work sites frequently featured an abundance of laborers. A government study that analyzed about 200 WPA construction projects in

1939 found that they utilized nearly four times more people than did similar projects completed by private contractors.[9]

Another factor was that many WPA employees had little previous experience with the type of work they were asked to do. The agency trained new hires in equipment operation and other skills, but it took time before a trainee could equal the productivity of an experienced worker. Older WPA workers also did not necessarily have the strength or stamina to perform physical labor at a high level for hours on end. Restrictions on hours that an individual could work each week further diminished their level of productivity. These limitations contributed to the revolving cast of laborers at many sites.

Finally, WPA construction crews often lacked advanced equipment to carry out jobs more quickly. Sponsoring groups were often reluctant to take on the expense of buying or renting those types of equipment. In addition, WPA administrators recognized that heavy use of such machinery would reduce the need for manpower.

"When people talk about, you know, leaning on the shovel, well, we did a whole lot of work. And a whole lot of hard work," remembered a man who built roads with the WPA in North Carolina.

Given all of these factors, it is not surprising that the average WPA construction project moved at a slower pace than similar private-sector sector job sites. The longer time frames involved had an impact on the overall expense of the projects. According to one government survey, it cost approximately 13 percent more to build a project through the WPA than it did to use a private contractor.[10] The quality of the work completed by the agency was found to be high, however, as judged by several reports on its construction practices. This finding indicates that the work-relief employees were not the incompetent shirkers described by critics.

Despite the limitations it faced, the WPA established an impressive list of construction accomplishments. Because local governments were so short of funds during the Depression, the WPA became the driving force for building and maintaining public infrastructure throughout the country, and the agency took on a broad range of tasks during its years of operation.

Road Construction

The building and repair of highways, roads, and city streets was the most common type of construction undertaken by the WPA. These projects could

The San Antonio River Walk

In 1938 city leaders in San Antonio, Texas, submitted an ambitious proposal to the WPA to revitalize a 2.5-mile section of the downtown area fronting the San Antonio River. The plan was largely the idea of architect Robert H. H. Hugman, who envisioned the creation of an elaborate waterfront walkway, complete with bridges, park-like landscaping, and access to shops and restaurants. Construction on Hugman's "River Walk" began in 1939 and was completed two years later.

The meandering, tree-shaded River Walk was as attractive as Hugman had promised. It was graced by extensive stonework, dozens of stairways, and even a waterside stage for theatrical performances. Nonetheless, critics soon deemed it a useless folly. Few people visited, commercial development languished, and it became an unsafe place to stroll after nightfall.

Ultimately, however, the architect's dream became a reality. Following a renovation project in the late 1960s, the River Walk developed into one of the state's top tourist attractions. It helped to spark an economic resurgence in the downtown area and the city as a whole, and it is now universally regarded as one of San Antonio's most vibrant and popular destinations.

easily make use of a large number of unskilled laborers and did not require a great deal of preliminary engineering work. Just as importantly, the nation urgently needed better roads. The number of automobiles on American roadways had increased dramatically in the 1920s, and in many parts of the country existing road networks were overwhelmed.

In urban areas, the WPA relieved automobile congestion by widening existing streets to allow them to handle more traffic. It also built new connecting thoroughfares to ease "bottlenecks" (points of traffic congestion) and improve traffic flow. In total, the agency built or improved 67,000 miles of city streets. On many of these WPA street construction projects, workers also built new sidewalks. The "WPA" initials stamped in walkway concrete became a familiar sight to several generations of Americans, and they can still be seen in some communities.

The WPA had an even greater impact on road systems in rural areas. With the exception of major highways, most roads between towns were in very poor shape in the mid-1930s. The difficulty of getting from place to place left some communities quite isolated. The WPA's work went a long way toward changing that, as agency employees built or improved a total of 572,000 miles of country roads. An important part of this effort involved building "farm-to-market" routes that were designed to better connect agricultural producers to population centers. Often, these roads were topped with gravel rather than a hard surface, but they nonetheless represented a marked improvement. These new and improved roadways not only aided in agricultural commerce, they gave rural Americans greater access to urban-based employment, education, and entertainment options. Congressman Sam Rayburn of Texas commented that "farm-to-market roads … changed the life of Texas farmers and ranchers."[11] Similar testimonials to the importance of these road improvements also were heard in other parts of the country.

Municipal Improvements

In addition to its work on city streets, the WPA tackled a wide range of other projects in urban areas, including improvements to sewage and water systems. Many cities desperately needed upgrades in these areas. In addition, such work could more easily be completed in winter than many other construction tasks. This consideration helped keep WPA employees busy when other projects were suspended for the winter months. The long list of achievements in this area included the installation or improvement of nearly 20,000 miles of water lines and 24,000 miles of sewers across the United States, as well as the construction or improvement of some 2,000 sewage or water treatment plants.

Parks and other recreation-related projects also figured prominently in the WPA story. Although workers created some parks from scratch, they also improved existing green space—often by adding features such as swimming pools, tennis courts, and golf courses. New York City saw many projects of this kind. Parks commissioner Robert Moses succeeded in getting so many projects approved that he frequently had tens of thousands of WPA employees labor-

Cove Creek High School in North Carolina was a WPA construction project

ing in the city at one time. In total, the WPA carried out more than 8,000 park creation or renovation projects around the country. In addition, the WPA built thousands of stadiums, grandstands, and athletic fields and nearly 13,000 playgrounds, more than half of which were located at public schools.

Public Buildings

Another important sector of WPA work involved the creation and reno-vation of government offices, schools, and other public buildings. These com-plex undertakings often required detailed engineering plans and significant con-tributions of skilled labor from carpenters, bricklayers, plumbers, stone masons, and other tradesmen. Many of these reinforced concrete structures were built according to a sleek, geometric visual arts design known as art deco that was immensely popular in the 1930s and 1940s.

The art deco design style was well suited to the purposes and resources of the WPA. The absence of ornate decoration meant that fewer skilled workers were needed in the construction process, and the minimalist design was usually cheaper to build and to maintain. Designers also made an effort to employ local materials as much as possible to keep costs low, which served the dual purpose of creating structures that fit well with the local surroundings.

All told, the WPA constructed 40,000 buildings and made improvements to 85,000 others. In addition to the schools and government offices mentioned above, the agency built or renovated fire stations, hospitals, military facilities, community buildings, libraries, auditoriums, gymnasiums, and prison buildings. Most of these projects were economical, attractive, and durable, and some are still in service today.

On occasion, WPA workers took on more unusual building projects. One of the most remarkable was Timberline Lodge, a publicly owned hotel for skiers that was built high atop Mount Hood in Oregon. Construction commenced in June 1936 and continued for the better part of two years, even through fierce weather that battered the mountain in winter time. Ultimately, Timberline became a grand showpiece that incorporated stone, timbers, and cedar-shake shingles as well as handcrafted furniture and interior decorations fashioned by WPA craftspeople. The lodge is now a National Historic Landmark and continues to serve its original function as a hotel. Workers also undertook the restoration and repair of historic structures. Among the locations to benefit from this work were the Antietam Civil War battlefield and Fort McHenry, both located in Maryland, and Mission San José, a church compound in San Antonio, Texas, that dates to the 1700s.

The WPA even built airports. With the growth of commercial aviation in the 1920s and early 1930s, U.S. cities began to feel the need to create or expand airport facilities. They subsequently approached the WPA with ambitious airport construction or remodeling plans. The execution of these plans did not always go smoothly for the WPA. Early on, in fact, some of the airports built by the agency suffered from poor planning. To remedy this problem, the WPA established a special section to oversee its aviation projects and received guidance from the federal agencies charged with regulating air travel.

Altogether, the agency worked on more than 1,000 airports—including 350 facilities that the WPA built from scratch. One of the largest and most

Building Utopia

Children play on the streets of Greendale, Wisconsin, 1939.

The WPA provided the manpower for one of the New Deal's most idealistic projects: construction of three "greenbelt" towns that were intended to serve as models of efficient urban planning and cooperative living. The idea for these communities came from Rexford Tugwell, director of the Resettlement Administration (RA). Tugwell's idea was to build entirely new towns on the edge of large metropolitan areas for people of low and moderate incomes. Each would include a large amount of green space to provide more pleasant and healthful surroundings than typically found in the nation's cities. Plans were drawn up for three of these communities—Greenbelt (in Maryland), Greenhills (Ohio), and Greendale (Wisconsin)—and in 1935 WPA

important was LaGuardia Airport in New York City, which was built over a two-year period from 1937 to 1939 at a total cost of $40 million. The expertise the agency developed in airport construction became especially valuable as World War II loomed, and the WPA became heavily involved in building military airfields after the United States entered the conflict in December 1941.

Conservation Projects and Disaster Response

During the life of the WPA, the agency even delved into major water control and land conservation projects that resembled programs carried out during the Depression by the Civilian Conservation Corps (CCC) and the Public Works Administration (PWA). When the Midwest was wracked by drought conditions in the mid-1930s, for example, WPA officials approved numerous dam-building projects. These structures did not approach the magnitude of the major dams built by the PWA, such as the Hoover and Grand Coulee dams. The con-

work crews began transforming empty land into Tugwell's vision of a model city. The towns that took shape shared a common design. Houses were situated to take advantage of the park-like surroundings, while businesses, schools, and a community facility were located in a town center. The cities even made an effort to minimize automobile traffic by incorporating extensive walking paths.

The federal government owned all property in these communities, and it leased houses to families at specified rates. All businesses were cooperatively owned, and the individuals who sought to live in the towns were carefully screened in regard to income, family members, and even personal behavior. The screening process for residency was designed to create a peaceful and cohesive community, but this strict oversight had strong socialist overtones. Critics bestowed Tugwell with the nickname of "Rex the Red"—red being a color strongly associated with the socialist and communist political philosophies. The greenbelt initiative's philosophical underpinnings made the communities increasingly controversial, and in the early 1950s the federal government sold off the property to private owners under pressure from conservatives. Today, however, the communities continue to be popular residential areas, and they still retain much of their distinctive design and historic architecture.

crete dams and earthen (made of compacted earth) dams the WPA took on were much smaller affairs. Even small dams could be challenging projects, however, as the agency discovered when several of its earliest dam building efforts failed due to poor design and planning. These collapses convinced the WPA to get approval for all dam designs from the United States Engineering Office before beginning work on the project.

Other conservation projects completed by the WPA included planting trees to prevent soil erosion and building firebreaks and fire towers to help prevent forest fires. In addition, WPA work crews played an important role in reducing water pollution in the nation's coal-producing regions. They sealed abandoned mine shafts to prevent sulfuric acid from leaching into area waterways.

Finally, the WPA's construction capabilities and its ability to mobilize large numbers of workers on short notice made the agency a major asset in responding to floods, hurricanes, tornadoes, and other natural disasters. When these

Among the many WPA works built in Texas was the Possum Kingdom Stone Arch Bridge, which spans the state's Brazos River. The bridge is the longest and most substantial masonry arch bridge in Texas.

calamities struck American communities, WPA personnel took on tasks such as constructing levees to help control flooding, evacuating residents, performing emergency repairs on bridges, and transporting supplies of food and water.

When the Mississippi and Ohio Rivers flooded in January 1937, for example, WPA laborers swooped in and provided desperately needed assistance to traumatized communities up and down those waterways. "Braving cold winds, rain, snow and sleet, WPA crews worked throughout the flood at jobs hazardous and unpleasant, mostly in cold and water," wrote the *Evansville Courier,* a newspaper in Indiana:

> They were everywhere, from start to finish, doing all kinds of
> jobs—constructing sanitary toilets over sewer manholes to pro-

tect the city's health, carrying relief supplies over precarious cat-walks, cooking and serving meals for refugees, soldiers and coast guardsmen, disposing of garbage and refuse, rescuing livestock and persons.... The end of the flood, like the beginning, found them in action, cleaning up debris deposited on city streets and county roads.[12]

A Blue-Collar Army

Over the course of the WPA's existence from 1935 to 1943, the agency provided construction-related jobs for 6.5 million Americans—77 percent of the WPA's total work force. As a result, WPA's blue-collar construction workers became symbolic of the agency as a whole. They also made a strong impression on the public consciousness because of the sheer number of WPA construction projects that popped up all across the country from the mid-1930s through the early 1940s. Indeed, signs emblazoned with the words "USA, Work Program, WPA" became a common sight in big cities and rural areas alike.

The charges of loafing and shovel-leaning that dogged WPA construction projects never completely went away. The legacy of new and improved streets, sewage systems, bridges, libraries, firehouses, parks, and schools left behind by WPA work crews, however, is an extensive and impressive one. Defenders of the WPA assert that the projects made a positive impact in nearly every community—and that they continued to benefit multiple generations of Americans long after the agency closed its doors.

Notes

[1] Quoted in Watkins, T. H. *The Hungry Years: A Narrative History of the Great Depression in America.* New York: Holt, 1999, p. 262.

[2] Roosevelt, Franklin D. *The Public Papers and Addresses of Franklin D. Roosevelt,* Vol. 4. New York: Random House, 1938, p. 137.

[3] Roosevelt, p. 135.

[4] Quoted in McElvaine, Robert S., ed. *Down and Out in the Great Depression: Letters from the "Forgotten Man."* Chapel Hill: University of North Carolina Press, 1983, p. 128.

[5] Quoted in Ginzberg, Eli. *The Unemployed.* Edited by Ben B. Seligman. 1943. Reprint. New Brunswick, NJ: Transaction, 2004, p. 70.

[6] Quoted in Ginzberg, p. 66.

[7] Quoted in Ginzberg, pp. 70-71.

[8] Quoted in Taylor, Nick. *American Made: The Enduring Legacy of the WPA: When FDR Put the Nation to Work.* New York: Bantam, 2008, pp. 366-67.

[9] *Security, Work, and Relief Policies: Report of the Committee on Long-Range Work and Relief Policies to the National Resources Planning Board.* Washington, DC: U.S. Government Printing Office, 1942, p. 247.

[10] *Security, Work, and Relief Policies,* p. 247.

[11] Quoted in Edsforth, Ronald. *The New Deal: America's Response to the Great Depression.* Malden, MA: Blackwell, 2000, p. 222.

[12] Quoted in "Ohio River Flood of 1937." From *Work Relief under John K. Jennings, 1931-1939,* n.d. The Lilly Library, Indiana University. Retrieved from http://www.indiana.edu/~liblilly/wpa/flood.html.

Chapter Five

THE WPA ARTS, SERVICE, WOMEN'S, AND YOUTH PROGRAMS

———◦⊸◦———

It was like winning a lottery for ten million dollars.... We couldn't believe that you got paid *steady,* twenty-three dollars a week just to paint. It was the craziest thing we ever heard of.[1]

—Artist Herman Cherry remembering the launch of the Federal Art Project

Construction was the primary focus of the WPA, but the agency did employ individuals in other types of work. Generally described as "service projects," these non-construction endeavors helped fulfill two ideals championed by the WPA leadership: 1) all unemployed workers deserved an opportunity to earn their financial assistance, and 2) as much as possible, WPA enrollees should be employed in fields in which they had skill and experience.

The service project initiative was also motivated by the need to reach out to unemployed women, who were excluded from construction work, and to young Americans struggling to find their first jobs. To carry out all of these efforts, WPA administrators took an imaginative approach to job creation and pursued a diverse range of work projects. Many of these projects, however, further heightened the controversy surrounding work-relief programs of the New Deal era.

Saving Starving Artists

The best-known WPA efforts to assist non-blue collar workers consisted of a group of programs that employed painters, sculptors, actors, writers, musicians, and other creative artists. Although President Roosevelt backed these initiatives, the most enthusiastic White House supporter was first lady Eleanor

First lady Eleanor Roosevelt strongly supported work relief programs for artists, writers, and musicians.

Roosevelt. The first lady, in fact, offered input on the operation of the programs, lobbied her husband on their behalf, and helped defend and promote them in radio and newspaper interviews. WPA director Harry Hopkins, too, backed the effort. When questioned as to why the WPA was offering support to artists, he had a simple answer: "Hell, they've got to eat just like other people."[2]

Hopkins's plainspoken justification for the arts programs only told part of the story, though. Supporters also argued that the inexpensive entertainment and cultural enrichment provided by WPA artists could lift public spirits at a time when few people could afford to attend shows, concerts, or museums. In addition, advocates believed that these initiatives would help spur a cultural renaissance and make the creative arts a more prominent part of life for all Americans. Some even hoped that the WPA programs would develop into a permanent federal agency to support cultural affairs.

The idea of greatly increasing the government's role in the arts was not universally embraced, however. The WPA's arts projects figured prominently in debates over the political agenda of the Roosevelt administration, and they ultimately became high-profile targets for opponents of the New Deal. This uproar was all the more striking given that these programs were actually a very small part of the WPA's overall operations. They accounted for about 1 percent of the agency's budget and employed a tiny fraction of its total work force.

The WPA established several distinct arts programs that were organized within a special division of the agency known as Federal Project Number One, or more commonly Federal One. The art programs were not required to have a local sponsoring group, as was the case with other WPA projects. As a result, they were almost entirely financed by the federal government, although small amounts of money were raised for some programs through ticket sales and other forms of public support. WPA leaders understood that local governments and other groups would not be able to spend money on artistic undertakings at a time when public funds were in such short supply. The drawback to this arrangement was that it gave critics an opening to portray the arts programs as wasteful Washington boondoggles that churned out works that local communities did not need or want.

The Federal Art Project

Visual arts such as painting, graphics, and sculpture formed the basis of the Federal Art Project (FAP), which adopted an expansive approach to its mission. FAP not only hired artists to produce works, it also organized exhibits, community arts centers, and a historic survey of American design. Through these initiatives, the FAP sought to make art more accessible and relevant to a wider range of Americans.

Holger "Eddie" Cahill, a former museum curator from New York City, served as director of the FAP. Rather than follow the lead of previous New Deal arts programs, which had emphasized high-quality works and sometimes offered commissions to well-known artists, Cahill took a more democratic approach. He offered assignments to large numbers of artists, many of whom were relatively—and sometimes completely—unknown. The underlying idea was that the large quantity of artists would create a large quantity of work, which would help to make art a more integral part of society. These choices ensured a lot of employment opportunities, which remained the top priority of the entire WPA.

The artists who joined the FAP payroll produced a wide variety of works. Large-scale murals for public buildings became a very visible part of the agency's output. Approximately 2,500 public murals were produced during the life of FAP. As time passed, though, small paintings that could be produced on an easel emerged as the division's main focus. Federal One artists created 108,000 of these works, as well as nearly 19,000 pieces of sculpture. Graphic prints were another FAP specialty. Many of the 36,000 different poster designs created by the program were used to publicize other New Deal-related events or projects.

As time passed, the FAP increasingly resembled an art factory of sorts, and in certain cases the artists did labor in factory-like conditions. Many FAP painters and sculptors were required to report to specific studios, where their hours and output were closely monitored (see "A Young Artist Describes His Experiences with the WPA's Federal Art Project," p. 197). Other artists, however, were permitted to work unsupervised in their own homes or studios and to report their hours on the honor system. Cahill himself favored this latter approach.

WPA artists chiseling a mural onto a wall of the tropical bird house at the Audubon Park Zoo in New Orleans.

Regardless of the conditions they worked under, FAP artists were paid at roughly the same level as skilled construction workers in the WPA. For many artists, this level of compensation improved their standard of living. "Almost every artist I knew was more flush than they had ever been before,"[3] remembered sculptor and painter Reuben Kadish.

FAP's high-volume operation resulted in art of a rather uneven quality. Taken as a whole, though, the art generated through the program conveyed a strong sense of the era and the spirit of hopefulness and national unity that formed the foundation of the New Deal. Many of the artists employed by the project belonged to the social realism movement, which depicted the difficulties of daily life rather than images of idealized beauty. During a period when work—or lack of work—was a national preoccupation, they took a special interest in depictions of industrial workers and farm laborers, both of whom often appeared as heroic figures. FAP artists also displayed a strong interest in creating paintings, sculpture, and prints revolving around the American experience; artists often chose historic incidents or the characteristics of specific regions as the subjects for their work.

FAP also made an important contribution to American art simply by allowing large numbers of artists to continue developing their talents during a period when very few of them could have supported themselves through sales of their works. The artist Seymour Fogel, who became successful in the post-World War II era, noted that his work with FAP "not only saved my life financially but launched my career as an artist."[4] A number of other people on the FAP payroll later became respected and influential figures in American art as well, including Mark Rothko, Willem de Kooning, and Jackson Pollock (see Pollock biography, p. 141).

Federal Theatre Project

In opting to support the dramatic arts with the Federal Theatre Project (FTP), another of Federal One's divisions, the WPA took on a complex challenge. Whereas painters and sculptors only needed basic materials and a studio in which to work, theatrical productions usually involved large groups of actors and technicians, not to mention an actual theater stage on which to present the show. In addition to these financial and logistical considerations, the FTP courted controversy with some of its subject matter. Although the majority of its shows were mainstream fare—Shakespearean dramas, musicals, and children's entertainment—the FTP became better known for producing plays that had a confrontational character and tackled explosive contemporary issues. That approach often made for exciting theater and some of the most innovative art produced by the WPA, but it also made FTP a lightning rod for conservative New Deal critics.

The person who bore the brunt of this criticism was FTP director Hallie Flanagan, a

Hallie Flanagan provided visionary leadership to the WPA's Federal Theatre Project.

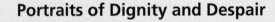

Portraits of Dignity and Despair

Some of the most iconic artwork produced during the New Deal came not from the WPA arts projects but from the Farm Security Administration (FSA), a federal agency created by the Roosevelt administration to assist struggling farmers. From 1937 to 1942, the FSA hired photographers to record the lives of agricultural workers, including the sharecroppers of the South and migrant families who had been uprooted from their ancestral homes by drought and economic hardship.

The FSA photography project benefited from the participation of a very strong group of photographers, among them Walker Evans, Gordon Parks, Russell Lee, and Dorothea Lange. In carrying out their assignments, these individuals spent long days on the road, traveling through small towns and migrant camps. During their travels, they experienced what Lange described as "hard, hard living ... not too far away from the people we were working

former college classmate of Harry Hopkins who later became the head of the drama program at Vassar College. She strongly believed that the theater could be "a social and educative force,"[5] and that it should challenge its audience and reflect the concerns of its community. That ideal was clearly evident in the "Living Newspaper" productions of the FTP, which dramatized aspects of current political and social issues (see "The FTP's 'Living Newspaper' Plays—Insightful Commentary or Government Propaganda?," p. 204).

The first Living Newspaper production, *Ethiopia*, began rehearsals in the fall 1935. It immediately demonstrated the level of controversy these shows could provoke. Senior members of the Roosevelt administration became concerned about the play's negative portrayal of the Italian fascist leader Benito Mussolini, and they decreed that all FTP scripts concerning foreign heads of

with." In 1936, Lange was wrapping up a month of work in California when she snapped one of the most famous of all Depression-era photos, "Migrant Mother, 1936." Years later, she described the circumstances that resulted in the famous photograph:

> I was following instinct, not reason; I dove into that wet and soggy camp and parked my car like a homing pigeon. I saw and approached the hungry and desperate mother as if drawn by a magnet. I do not remember how I explained my presence or my camera to her but I do remember she asked me no questions. I made five exposures, working closer and closer from the same direction. I did not ask her name or her history. She told me her age, that she was thirty-two. She said they had been living on frozen vegetables from the surrounding fields, and birds that the children had killed. She had just sold the tires from her car to buy food. There she sat in that lean-to tent with her children huddled around her, and seemed to know that my pictures might help her, and so she helped me. There was a sort of equality about it.

Source

Lange, Dorothea. "The Assignment I'll Never Forget: Migrant Mother." *Popular Photography,* February 1960, quoted in Kennedy, Roger G., and David Larkin. *When Art Worked.* New York: Rizzoli, 2009, p. 264.

state needed to be approved by the State Department. The play's director resigned in protest, and the show closed after a single dress-rehearsal performance. Later Living Newspaper plays were equally provocative, though they were staged without incident. These included *AAA Plowed Under* (about New Deal agricultural reforms that had been blocked by the Supreme Court), *One-Third of a Nation* (which tackled slum housing and unemployment in America's cities), and *Power* (dramatizing the efforts of the Tennessee Valley Authority to bring electricity to the rural South).

Other FTP productions centered on political issues as well. The most famous of them all was *The Cradle Will Rock*, a musical directed by Orson Welles (see Welles biography, p. 150) and produced by John Houseman. Both of these men later became famous members of America's entertainment industry. The

Actress Olive Stanton (who was homeless before hiring on with the WPA) stands next to a poster for *The Cradle Will Rock.*

play's pro-labor depiction of a steel-mill strike was set to debut in New York in June 1937, in the immediate aftermath of violent labor unrest in several U.S. cities. Just days before the curtain was scheduled to rise, however, WPA officials in Washington announced that no new plays or other presentations would be allowed to open that month. Agency officials blamed budget cutbacks for the cancellation, but many observers believed that *The Cradle Will Rock* was shut down because of its clear support for unions and its hostile characterization of American corporations. Although the company was locked out of its Broadway theater, Welles, Houseman, and their collaborators decided to perform the show anyway. They subsequently carried out a bare-bones performance of the play in another theater—an act of defiance that focused additional media attention on the production (see "An Actor in the Federal Theatre Project Recalls the Staging of *The Cradle Will Rock,*" p. 201).

The ongoing controversy swirling around the FTP highlighted some key issues related to government-funded arts projects. The first was censorship. Hopkins had promised that the FTP would be allowed to present "free, uncensored, adult theatre,"[6] but the events surrounding *Ethiopia* and *The Cradle Will Rock* indicated that the government sometimes attempted to control the content of the art it funded. To those who placed a high value on free speech, such interference cast doubt on the entire concept of having public agencies oversee creative art. A related concern involved the pro-New Deal stance of some of the FTP productions. Roosevelt's political opponents charged that these shows were, in effect, propaganda pieces that used taxpayer dollars to promote the president's policies. The political debate over the FTP escalated to a new level when conservative members of Congress began to allege that some members of the FTP were not merely liberal supporters of the president but radical leftists intent on sowing communist ideas in American society.

Federal One Programs for Writers and Musicians

Allegations of radical infiltration also swirled around the Federal Writers' Project (FWP), the Federal One program for writers hit hard by the Depression. These accusations, however, had more to do with the political views and activities of individuals in certain FWP offices than with the actual material they generated.

FWP writers took on two major tasks: creating travel guidebooks and collecting and publishing works that documented America's past, including oral histories, folklore, and traditional ballads. The FWP published travel guides for all forty-eight states (Hawaii and Alaska had not yet been awarded statehood), as well as titles focusing on specific cities, regions, and historic routes. The books explored even the most remote parts of the country in great detail, providing information on each area's history, economy, and culture. This bounty of information was supplemented with standard guidebook features about local attractions and driving itineraries. Many of the books became popular and widely respected resources for travelers, and a sizeable number of them were reprinted in new editions through the decades.

The songs, folktales, and personal narratives collected by FWP workers also provided historically useful chronicles of American culture. Perhaps the most valuable of these undertakings was a project to interview several thousand African Americans who had worked as slaves in the 1800s. By recording the experiences of these individuals before they passed away, the FWP preserved eyewitness accounts of an important and seldom-studied (at the time) aspect of U.S. history. The FWP also nurtured the talents of a number of writers who later become important figures in American literature, including Richard Wright, Eudora Welty, Kenneth Rexroth, Ralph Ellison, and Saul Bellow.

The Federal Music Project (FMP) was one of the most broad-ranging of the WPA arts programs. It encompassed both classical fare and popular genres of music, and it placed a strong emphasis on music education. The classical endeavors were closest to the heart of the project's director, Nikolai Sokoloff, an accomplished violinist and orchestra conductor. Under his direction, the FMP established thirty-four new symphony orchestras in its first year and a half of operation, and several of those ensembles continued to perform long after the WPA came to an end.

On a personal level, Sokoloff had little use for non-classical forms of music. He had a professional obligation, though, to put large numbers of musicians to work and provide cash-strapped and demoralized American families and communities with low-cost entertainment. He thus set his personal preferences aside and welcomed diverse artists onto the WPA payroll, including swing musicians, cowboy balladeers, and small ensembles that played traditional Hispanic and country music. Free or modestly priced shows given by FMP performers (and publicized through posters produced by the Federal Art Project) became common occurrences in towns and cities across the country, and they often drew large audiences. Some of these performances took place in concert halls, but FMP musicians also turned up in less formal settings, such as outdoor ice-skating rinks and train stations.

The busiest years for the Federal Music Project were between 1935 and 1939. During that four-year span, musicians employed by FMP presented 224,000 performances across the country. About 150 million people attended these shows, and an even wider audience enjoyed the music by listening to recorded concerts broadcast over the radio. Moreover, the FMP music classes offered instruction to some 14 million students. Together, the project's performances and lessons—as well as related initiatives that included making copies of musical scores—made the FMP the largest employer among all Federal One divisions. At its peak in 1936, the program provided jobs for approximately 16,000 professional musicians.

The WPA Women's Division

Although men dominated the American work force of the 1920s, women remained a significant part of the labor market. They worked as teachers, social workers, nurses, librarians, housekeepers, textile factory workers, farm laborers, secretaries, and office clerks. According to the U.S. Census, one of every four workers in 1930 was female. Like their male counterparts, though, many of them lost their jobs during the Great Depression.

WPA officials recognized the need to assist unemployed women, but the agency had only limited success in this regard. The percentage of women hired by the WPA averaged just less than 16 percent during its first six years of operation, even though they constituted about 25 percent of the general work force. Several factors contributed to this anemic performance. WPA work programs gave hiring preference to the principal wage earner in each household, which in the case of married couples was usually the husband. Another obstacle was that many women who sought a WPA job also had the responsibility of caring for children, which made it difficult or impossible for them to work the hours specified. In addition, females who had not previously worked outside the home were often ineligible for WPA positions because the agency was primarily concerned with assisting individuals who had lost their private-sector jobs. Finally, most WPA hiring filled out construction crews, and these jobs were considered unsuitable for women. Finally, the agency had a mixed record of launching employment initiatives focused on women.

Ellen Woodward headed the WPA Women's Division from 1935 to 1938.

Ellen Woodward, the director of the Women's Division of the WPA, identified some 250 job categories that could be filled by women (see Woodward biography, p. 154). Her superiors, however, disqualified women from applying for most of these positions. As a result, the majority of women who went to work for the WPA were employed in a limited number of categories, many of which were tied to the traditional roles that women had filled as homemakers. For example, they played a prominent role in the agency's food programs, which provided lunches to schoolchildren and distributed canned goods and fresh produce to individuals in need. Women also played an instrumental role in programs that provided housekeeping and childcare assistance to families in times of emergency.

The single most common job filled by women, however, was that of seamstress. The agency established 9,000 sewing centers that produced clothing, blankets, and sheets for struggling households and public institutions such as hospitals. Women workers took on many clerical duties as well, particularly if they had previous experience in office work, and they led many adult education classes and nursery-school programs. One of the most equitable areas of the WPA was the Federal Art Project, where just over 40 percent of the workers were female.

Additional opportunities opened up for women in the final years of the WPA's existence. Beginning in July 1940, women began taking part in vocational training for industrial jobs tied to military manufacturing. This training helped

"Rosie the Riveter" became one of the most famous images of the World War II era—and an enduring symbol of strength and equality for women.

set the stage for large numbers of women to move into factory jobs during World War II, when many male workers served in the U.S. military. These women who served their country on the home front were famously depicted by the iconic figure of "Rosie the Riveter." Women made up a much larger proportion of the WPA payroll once America formally entered the war in December 1941. Men left the agency at a faster rate than women during the next few years to take jobs in private industry or join the armed forces. By December 1942, when the WPA began winding down its operations, two out of five of its employees were women.

National Youth Administration

All segments of American society struggled with the lack of employment opportunities during the Depression, but young people were especially hard hit. As the nation's economic difficulties deepened, many parents pressured their children to begin looking for work at an early age so that they could contribute to the household income. Countless young people had to abandon their schooling to do so. Economic hardship—and the family discord that often accompanied it—also spurred many youths to run away from home. A Department of Labor report from 1932 estimated that 200,000 children had become homeless tramps who largely relied on panhandling to survive. More commonly, the nation's impoverished young people remained with their families. But many of them still faced a bleak future, as their options for schooling or for learning a trade were very limited.

This state of affairs worried many Americans, including first lady Eleanor Roosevelt. She not only expressed alarm about the present hardships faced by young people, she also feared that their experiences might have a prolonged negative effect on their lives—and on the health and vitality of the nation as a whole. "We are going to have a generation of people who do not know how to work," Roosevelt wrote, "and who ignore our old standards of morals and ethics because they cannot live up to them."[7]

Mrs. Roosevelt lobbied her husband to take action on the issue. In June 1935 he created the National Youth Administration (NYA) by executive order and made it a part of the WPA. Aubrey Williams, a senior assistant to Harry Hopkins, was named as the agency's executive director. Williams guided an operation that had several goals: to provide jobs to men and women ages sixteen to twenty-five; to help those individuals who were enrolled in high school or college to continue with their studies; and to offer vocational job training and assistance in job placement. In some ways, the efforts of the NYA were similar to those of the Civilian Conservation Corps, but the NYA's state directors (including future president Lyndon B. Johnson—see Johnson biography, p. 133) took a more diverse approach. It served both men and women and put people to work in a variety of jobs, whereas the CCC had used all-male corps members on outdoor-oriented projects in remote locations.

Young people who participated in the NYA Student Aid Program were provided part-time jobs while remaining enrolled as students. High school students could earn up to $6 per month (about $100 in 2012 dollars), undergraduate college students as much as $20 (the equivalent of about $335) and graduate students a maximum of $40 (the equivalent of about $670). High schoolers were limited to a part-time schedule of no more than twenty-two hours per week, but college students could put in additional time on the job. NYA enrollees performed a wide range of work, including clerical duties, library work, and assignments as teachers' or nurses' aides.

The NYA Works Projects Program, on the other hand, assisted young men and women who were not enrolled in school. They could earn $25 per month (about $415 in 2012 dollars) while putting in as many as seventy hours a month on the job. Men taking part in this program often performed labor on construction projects, while women usually received assignments to serve as aides in office, library, school, or hospital environments. NYA provided vocational training in skills such as carpentry, plumbing, and barbering. These programs were in high demand, since most apprenticeship training in these and other fields had dried up during the early years of the Depression.

Many men and women took part in NYA training while continuing to live at home, but others relocated to special residential facilities where they received

A Florida youth enrolled in NYA vocational training for work in the defense industry.

instruction and completed any associated work assignments. As the likelihood of war increased in the late 1930s, NYA vocational training increasingly focused on skills that could be used in industries related to military equipment and materials, and the men and women who received this instruction played a valuable role in the U.S. war effort.

African Americans in the NYA and other WPA Programs

The National Youth Administration made a determined effort to include African-American youth in its programs. The agency's success in this regard stemmed from the leadership of Mary McLeod Bethune, who headed the NYA Office of Negro Affairs (see Bethune biography, p. 121). Some 300,000 blacks took part in youth administration programs, and the NYA extended aid to African Americans in numbers that equaled and sometimes exceeded their percentage of the general population. Although the agency could not break the codes of racial segregation that held sway in the South, even in that region of the country the NYA broke new ground by promoting blacks into administrative positions and by insisting that blacks be paid the same wages as white participants. Moreover, vocational training programs helped African Americans move into skilled and semi-skilled jobs in larger numbers during the 1930s.

Bethune was an outspoken advocate for the black men and women who were aided by these programs, as well as the overall NYA mission. "I believe it to be one of the most stabilizing projects for the benefit of the Americans of tomorrow, than possibly any one thing we have done,"[8] she said in 1936.

Outside of the NYA, the WPA did not have a specific division devoted to African Americans or other minorities. However, Hopkins and other WPA officials did make a concerted effort to insure that the benefits of work relief were extended to large numbers of black workers. An average of about 350,000 African Americans were on the WPA payroll each year during the late 1930s. They accounted for about 15 percent of the agency's work force at a time when blacks made up only about 10 percent of America's citizenry. When the Urban League assessed the WPA's track record in hiring minorities, the organization noted that "discrimination on various projects because of race have been kept to a minimum and ... in almost every community Negroes have been given a chance to participate in the work program."[9] In the majority of cases, the WPA provided equal pay to blacks—which was rarely the case in the private sector—and it offered them opportunities for advancement and training in skilled positions.

The agency was not completely free of racial bias, though. Some projects, particularly those in the South, were plagued by discrimination in hiring and unequal treatment of blacks who were granted jobs. There was also a tendency throughout the country to relegate African Americans to the low-paying unskilled positions on WPA job sites. But compared with the treatment minorities received in American society as a whole in the 1930s, the WPA was a progressive force that played an important part in the Roosevelt administration's efforts to promote greater racial equality.

The severe hardship experienced by blacks during the Depression made the assistance provided by the agency all the more valuable, and the WPA's achievements were widely appreciated among the African-American population.

"The WPA came along and Roosevelt came to be a god," remembered one black whose community benefited from the agency's operations. "It was really great. You worked, you got a paycheck, and you had some dignity."[10] The minority hiring carried out by the WPA and other New Deal work-relief programs became a primary factor in the president's strong support from black voters.

Although individuals from other minority groups were involved in the WPA as well, the agency maintained few detailed statistics on these workers. The government's final report on the agency noted that people whose ethnicity was identified as "other"—meaning not white or black—ranged from 0.4 to 0.6 percent of the WPA work force in the period between 1939 and 1942.[11] Earlier statistics are not provided, and there is no attempt to identify the members of the "other" category by specific group, such as Hispanic or Native American.

Many Jobs for Many People

WPA service projects employed far fewer people than the construction initiatives, but they still encompassed a huge range of jobs. In addition to the aforementioned work by Federal One, the NYA, and the Women's Division, WPA workers assisted cash-strapped libraries by repairing books and providing service to remote areas via bookmobiles and even horseback delivery. WPA employees also helped expand health services by conducting testing, immunizations, and other routine tasks under the direction of medical personnel, and they were particularly active in the push to provide better preventative care to children. In the area of research and recordkeeping, the agency provided employees to help conduct government surveys, studies, and general recordkeeping. Moreover, its Historical Records Survey carried out a thorough analysis and organization of public records in every county in the nation. This immense undertaking was extremely valuable in helping preserve the documentary record of the nation's history. WPA employees even oversaw recreation programs devoted to exercise, dance, and arts-and-crafts activities in American communities.

Service projects became more numerous in the agency's final years. The WPA became increasingly focused on defense-related projects after 1940, and the majority of these endeavors were classified as service work. In addition, female workers came to account for a larger percentage of the agency's work force during these last years, which led to an increased emphasis on jobs outside of the construction sector. By the agency's final months of operation in 1943, about three out of five WPA workers were engaged in non-construction work.

While the service projects accounted for only about one-quarter of the total WPA work-relief mission, these initiatives embodied some of the most progressive aspirations of the New Deal. The agency's efforts to support the arts community and to benefit women, youth, and minorities represented a bold new type of social activism on the part of government. In this regard, the WPA laid the groundwork for a wide range of post-World War II governmental programs focused on support for the arts, infrastructure development, social welfare, and public assistance to the poor.

Notes

[1] Quoted in Naifeh, Steven, and Gregory White Smith. *Jackson Pollock: An American Saga.* New York: Clarkson N. Potter, 1989, p. 268.

[2] Quoted in Watkins, T. H. *The Hungry Years: A Narrative History of the Great Depression in America.* New York: Holt, 1999, p. 275.

[3] Quoted in Naifeh, p. 277.

[4] Quoted in McKinzie, Richard D. *The New Deal for Artists.* Princeton, NJ: Princeton University Press, 1973, p. 176.

[5] Flanagan, Hallie. *Arena: The History of the Federal Theatre.* New York: Benjamin Blom, 1940, p. 54.

[6] Flanagan, p. 69.

[7] Quoted in Watkins, p. 268.

[8] Quoted in McClusky, Audrey Thomas, and Elaine M. Smith, eds. *Mary McLeod Bethune: Building a Better World.* Bloomington: Indiana University Press, 1999, p. 216.

[9] Quoted in Sitkoff, Harvard. "The New Deal and Race Relations." In *Fifty Years Later: The New Deal Evaluated.* Edited by Harvard Sitkoff. New York: Knopf, 1985, p. 100.

[10] Quoted in Turkel, Studs. *Hard Times: An Oral History of the Great Depression.* 1970. Reprint. New York: New Press, 1986, p. 437.

[11] *Final Report on the WPA Program 1935-43.* Washington, DC: U.S. Government Printing Office, 1947, p. 45.

Chapter Six

THE END OF THE WPA

It seems that the New Deal is working along hand in glove with the Communist Party. The New Deal is either for the Communist Party, or it is playing into the hands of the Communist Party.[1]

—U.S. representative J. Parnell Thomas

Please continue this W.P.A. program. It makes us feel like an American citizen to earn our own living.[2]

—A worker from Battle Creek, Michigan, writing to President Roosevelt, 1936

The Works Progress Administration (WPA) continued operating until the early 1940s, when America's military buildup for World War II at last brought about a full economic recovery that made the agency unnecessary. In its final years, though, the WPA underwent a number of important changes. President Franklin D. Roosevelt's desire to curb federal spending and reduce the nation's budget deficit accounted for some of these changes. An even bigger factor, however, was the political warfare between America's progressive and conservative camps in the late 1930s. These battles between supporters and opponents of the New Deal often focused on the issue of government-sponsored employment. As a result, the WPA became a prominent subject of discussion in the larger national debate over the Roosevelt presidency

An Unpopular Court-Packing Scheme

The widespread public support enjoyed by President Roosevelt peaked around the time of the 1936 presidential election. He won a second term in

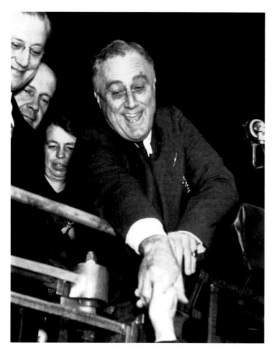

Franklin D. Roosevelt campaigning in Ohio in late 1936.

office by a huge landslide, claiming nearly 61 percent of the popular vote. Roosevelt thus entered his second term in 1937 with a strong mandate, but his popularity and prestige were greatly diminished in the months that followed.

The president's most damaging mistake was his unsuccessful effort to reform the U.S. judicial system and increase the number of justices on the U.S. Supreme Court. Roosevelt's so-called "court-packing" plan was motivated by the fact that the high court had struck down several important New Deal reforms as unconstitutional. These Supreme Court decisions angered and dismayed Roosevelt, who felt that several of the elderly Supreme Court justices were out of step with the nation.

Roosevelt subsequently decided that his administration—and the nation as a whole—needed a Supreme Court that would not be so hostile to the New Deal. The president asked Congress to pass a measure that would, among other things, allow him to appoint additional members to the court. Roosevelt's proposal would give him an opportunity to pack the Supreme Court with justices more likely to support his administration's various New Deal reforms. The plan immediately sparked a firestorm of criticism. Opponents called it a dangerous move that would upset the balance of power in the U.S. government and give Roosevelt and later presidents undue influence. Conservative Republicans even ascribed darker motives to the president's proposal. "The president's initiatives, his opponents maintained, proved that he was dangerously power hungry and that he aspired to be a dictator," wrote historian Richard Polenberg. "The charges, though wildly exaggerated, struck a responsive chord at a time when many Americans were troubled by the advance of dictatorships in Europe."[3]

Even Democratic members of Congress who had loyally supported the president in the past refused to get behind the controversial proposal. By the summer of 1937 the reform measure was dead, and Roosevelt had been dealt a resounding legislative defeat. The president's stubborn insistence on pushing the plan squandered the momentum he had enjoyed following his reelection. It also gave New Deal opponents renewed energy because they believed that public opinion was beginning to turn against the president.

The Roosevelt Recession

At the same time that the court-packing saga unfolded, Roosevelt moved to rein in government spending. He based his decision on positive signs that the economy was on the rebound. Unemployment levels, for example, had steadily declined. From 1936 to 1937, civilian unemployment fell from 9 million (17 percent of total labor force) to 7.7 million (14.3 percent). During this same period, corporations reported higher earnings and factories throughout the country increased production. The positive economic data convinced Roosevelt to rein in the deficit spending on which his administration had relied to revive the economy. The resulting budget cuts affected all of the New Deal programs that his administration had created to combat the effects of the Depression. The WPA lost $400 million in funding, which meant a reduction in the number of projects and jobs it could fund. Between January and December 1937, the agency's employment dropped by more than 500,000 people.

As 1937 unfolded, however, evidence accumulated that the Roosevelt administration's decision to cut spending on work programs and other economic stimulus was premature. As federal spending dropped, the economic recovery ran out of steam. In the fall of 1937, the nation experienced a painful reminder of the events that had precipitated the Depression eight years earlier. Demand for goods slowed, industrial production dropped, and unemployment levels began to rise again. Prices on the stock market went into a sudden nosedive on October 19. This market panic was quickly dubbed "Black Tuesday," like its predecessor in 1929.

By early 1938, the number of unemployed Americans had soared to nearly 10.4 million, wiping out most of the employment gains that had been made since 1935. Blame for the downturn, which came to be known as the "Roosevelt Recession," was laid at the president's door. Commentators argued that programs such as the WPA had helped spur economic activity and that the president should have waited to cut their funding until the economy had gained greater strength and stability.

Officials in the Roosevelt administration quickly decided that the faltering economy needed a fresh burst of spending on employment programs. In April 1938 the president asked Congress for $3 billion in increased funding, with much of the additional money to be allocated to the WPA and other work-relief programs. The House and Senate passed the measure, and the new financial resources allowed the WPA to greatly increase employment. By November 1938, the agency was providing jobs to more than 3.3 million people, which would prove to be the peak of WPA job creation. (From late 1935 until the middle of 1940, the agency's work force usually totaled between 2 and 3 million). Following the burst of government hiring in 1938, the economy began to improve. By 1939 national unemployment had dropped to about 9.5 million, and the United States was back on the path of a slow economic recovery that would continue into the early 1940s.

Patronage and Political Influence

The difficulties Roosevelt experienced in 1937 and 1938 inspired his political opponents to step up their attacks on the WPA. They intensified criticisms that they had lodged against the agency from the beginning. One of their most common complaints was that the Roosevelt administration used the agency as a means of gaining support for the president and for candidates who were friendly to the New Deal.

Patronage—the practice of politicians steering government jobs to specific individuals or districts in return for political support—had long been part of the American political process. Not surprisingly, it affected the WPA, an organization that controlled a large amount of money and jobs and that collaborated with public officials at all levels of government. In fact, the legislation that created the WPA, the Emergency Relief Appropriation Act of 1935, helped insure that patronage would be an integral part of its operations. Members of the Democrat-controlled U.S. Senate added an amendment to the bill requiring the president to attain the advice and consent of that chamber before appointing any WPA staff person making more than $5,000 a year. In effect, this provision allowed senators from each state to direct the senior-level WPA jobs to people of their choosing. In most cases, they chose individuals who were well connected to their party's state political operation. These hand-picked officials subsequently made sure that the party exerted control over the WPA projects in each local community.

Patronage of that type was considered standard operating procedure by many elected officials. However, critics also alleged that supervisors sometimes pressured WPA workers to vote for Democratic candidates and to make financial contributions to the Democratic Party or risk losing their jobs. Although overtly corrupt practices were limited, they did occur in some local areas. In New Jersey, for example, Jersey City mayor Frank Hague exerted complete control over WPA projects in the area. Hague used the government-funded jobs as an important tool of his political "machine," and he required employees in the WPA and other New Deal programs to contribute a percentage of their salaries to the Democratic Party.

Jersey City mayor Frank Hague became a symbol of WPA corruption to New Deal critics.

Roosevelt and the WPA national leadership did not condone such "kick-back" schemes. In 1936, for example, WPA director Harry Hopkins pointedly reminded WPA supervisors and employees that according to the agency's official policy, "no person shall be employed or discharged by the Works Progress Administration on the ground of his support or nonsupport of any candidate of any political organization."[4]

To help combat charges of political corruption as well as other types of wrongdoing, the WPA Division of Investigation was established in October 1935. Its efforts helped prevent any large-scale scandals from marring the WPA record, and historian Nick Taylor contends that "the WPA was demonstrably not corrupt on the national level."[5] The division's actions were limited, however. Hague and other powerful figures continued to run their local operations as they wished.

New Deal critics frequently cited Hague's involvement with the WPA as evidence that the Roosevelt administration directed WPA funds to specific cities and states to reward political supporters or to seek support from voters. For instance, Jersey City received $50 million in funding during Roosevelt's first two terms. This generous level of aid likely stemmed from the strong support that Hague showed for the president. Moreover, strong evidence exists that the WPA served as a "get out the vote" tool for Democrats in several tightly contested elections in various parts of the country. In those instances, WPA administrators launched new projects in the area in question shortly before voters went to the polls, with the expectation that grateful citizens would support the Democratic ticket (see "Herbert Hoover Condemns the Works Progress Administration," p. 208).

The Hunt for Radicals

Although opponents of the New Deal failed to gain much leverage with their complaints about WPA patronage, they experienced greater success in attacking the agency as a hotbed of radical leftists. Conservative critics had long charged that Roosevelt's policies were undermining the political, economic, and social foundations on which the nation rested. While only the more extreme critics truly believed that the president himself was trying to bring about a socialist revolution, the accusation that Roosevelt's *programs* had been taken over by people with revolutionary aims proved an effective weapon against the president and his policies.

U.S. representative Martin Dies of Texas led the charge on this front (see Dies biography, p. 125). A conservative Southern Democrat, Dies turned against the New Deal in the mid-1930s. He also gained national attention during this period for his warnings about communist subversion in the United States. In May 1938 he was appointed chair of the newly formed House Un-American Activities Committee (HUAC), which was originally intended to examine possible internal security threats in the United States. HUAC was charged with investigating not only "un-American" individuals and groups with communist and Socialist beliefs, but also Fascist and pro-Nazi groups in the United States. Under Dies's direction, however, the committee paid little attention to right-wing extremists,. Instead, HUAC focused on allegations of communist activity in America. Shortly after its investigative hearings began in the summer of 1938, the committee turned its attention to WPA—and to the Federal One arts programs in particular.

The provocative plays of the Federal Theatre Project (FTP) served as an inviting target for Dies and other conservative HUAC members. While backers of the arts programs may have seen the FTP dramas about labor unrest and New Deal reform as a vital source of social commentary, conservative members of HUAC framed them in much different terms. "Practically every play presented ... is sheer propaganda for Communism or the New Deal,"[6] declared Republican representative J. Parnell Thomas of New Jersey, who became a close ally of Dies in attacking the arts programs. The committee heard testimony from

Representative Martin Dies oversaw congressional investigations into the programs and activities of the WPA.

a number of witnesses who alleged that the FTP was riddled with communists, that those employed on the project in New York City were required to join a pro-communist organization, and that a general "un-American atmosphere"[7] thrived in the FTP production companies.

As time went on, Dies and many other HUAC members aired a range of sensational accusations, few of which were backed up by verifiable facts. The committee also became infamous for discouraging testimony from anyone who might refute the charges that had been made. Nonetheless, newspapers gave ample coverage to the biased hearings. These stories heightened public concern about the WPA and the New Deal in general.

The operations of the Federal Writers' Project (FWP) also received close scrutiny from HUAC. In this instance, allegations that a sizable number of the staff were supporters of radical political causes or groups had some justification. In New York City and San Francisco, in particular, communist-oriented factions became powerful forces in the local FWP offices. Their presence reduced the productivity of these offices, as rival political groups spent excessive amounts of time harassing one another over the fine points of ideology rather than completing their work. The radicalized members of the FWP and other arts projects were also prone to staging strikes and protests. These work stoppages usually stemmed from unhappiness with low wages or employee terminations due to agency budget cuts. These incidents were fairly limited in number, however, as administrators defused many of the conflicts by instituting changes in the agency's pay structure. Nonetheless, conservative opponents of the New Deal viewed the strikes as more proof that the agency was riddled with radical agitators.

The damage inflicted by the HUAC investigations was heightened by WPA administrators who initially ignored the public allegations made before the Dies committee. They believed the issue would soon fade away. When that failed to happen, the WPA issued statements to refute the charges, but the delayed response received little attention in the press. The agency's most spirited defense came when Hallie Flanagan of the FTP testified in the HUAC hearings in December 1938, along with two other senior officials. Their attempts to defend the WPA before hostile questioning had little effect in changing HUAC's opinion of arts programs, however. When the committee presented its report to the full U.S. House of Representative on January 3, 1939, it stated that:

> We are convinced that a rather large number of the employees on the Federal Theater Project are either members of the Communist Party or are sympathetic with the Communist Party. It is also clear that certain employees felt under compulsion to join the Workers' Alliance of America [a leftist labor organization with ties to the Communist Party] in order to retain their positions. The evidence is very clear that certain employees carried on communistic activities openly in the Federal Writers' Project.[8]

Overhauling the WPA

The HUAC investigations intensified congressional opposition to the WPA, and a strong Republican showing in the 1938 elections further strengthened Roosevelt's adversaries. The Republicans gained seventy-five seats in the House of Representatives and seven in the Senate. These results represented the first clear electoral proof that public support for the New Deal was waning. The 76th Congress that convened in January 1939 was still controlled by Democrats, but the increased number of Republicans joined forces with conservative Democrats to oppose the more liberal elements of Roosevelt's program, including the WPA.

Their efforts culminated in the passage of the Emergency Relief Appropriation Act of 1939, which Roosevelt reluctantly signed. This new law forced the WPA to make a broad range of operational changes. In terms of money, $125 million in WPA funding was reallocated to the Public Works Administration. The WPA's traditionally flexible approach to project funding also changed. Emergency Relief Appropriation Act provisions required sponsors to pay at least 25 percent of the bill.

Anti-New Deal congressman Clifton Woodrum, who had proclaimed that "I want the Federal Government to get out of the theater business," was delighted when the FTP was abolished.

The law also revised WPA employment regulations. Concerned that some workers had become too dependent on work relief, the architects of the Emergency Relief Appropriation Act included a provision that limited WPA employment to no more than eighteen months of continuous employment. This rule was applied retroactively, meaning that it applied to the employment records of WPA workers prior to the signing of the law. As a result, the WPA was forced to terminate the employment of 775,000 people who reached their eighteen-month limit in July and August of 1939. Moreover, the shift to a standard 130-hour month for all WPA workers took place at this time. This change forced many of the agency's workers to put in more hours for the same pay.

The uproar over the allegations of radical activity resulted in several other changes as well. All WPA workers were required to sign an oath stating their loyalty to the U.S. government, and all non-citizens became ineligible for employment with the agency. Significant alterations also were made to the arts programs. The Federal Theatre Project was simply abolished. The shuttering of the FTP delighted critics like anti-New Deal congressman Clifton Woodrum, who had proclaimed that "I want the Federal Government to get out of the theater business."[9]

The Federal Art, Writers', and Music Projects remained alive, but they underwent significant changes. The exemption that had enabled these groups

Killing Pinocchio

While the demise of the Federal Theatre Project was not a complete surprise given the attacks that had been aimed at it, its end came suddenly. As a result of the passage of the Emergency Relief Appropriation Act of 1939—the funding bill that killed the Federal Theatre Project—June 30 became the final day of operations for the program. Many of the companies with plays in production marked their farewell in a suitably dramatic manner. This was particularly true of the New York production of *Pinocchio*, which up to that point had been a popular and noncontroversial adaptation of the children's tale. On its final night, however, the company made the title character into a metaphor for the FTP. Rather than being transformed into a living boy, Pinocchio ended the play as a dead puppet. As the cast recited the lines, "Let us now proclaim our grief / that his small life was all too brief," he was laid in a casket emblazoned with the words "Killed by act of Congress, June 30 1939." Stagehands then brought the play to a destructive finale by tearing down the set in front of the audience. The reaction of the children attending the performance was not reported.

Source

Flanagan, Hallie. *Arena: The History of the Federal Theatre.* New York: Benjamin Blom, 1940, reissue 1965, p. 365.

to be wholly funded by the federal government was ended, meaning that all their work was now required to have a local or state sponsor who would cover the proscribed 25 percent of costs. This fundamental shift was reflected in new names for each group: they were rebranded as the WPA Art Program, Writers' Program, and Music Program.

At about the same time that the WPA was dealing with the reforms specified in the Emergency Relief Appropriation Act of 1939, it faced other changes as well. Congress approved a reorganization of the executive branch of the government that had been requested by President Roosevelt. The WPA thus became part of the Federal Works Agency, and its name was changed from the Works Progress Administration to the Work *Projects* Administration. The major functions of the agency remained the same, but there was one major difference: the National Youth Administration was removed from WPA and became part of the newly created Federal Security Agency.

The WPA also experienced a major change in leadership as the 1930s drew to a close. Harry Hopkins resigned as the agency's director in late December 1938, after the president appointed him secretary of commerce. He was replaced by Colonel Francis C. Harrington, who had served with the United States Army Corps of Engineers for more than twenty-five years before joining the WPA Construction Division. Roosevelt's selection of the former military officer would soon prove prophetic, because the WPA was about to undertake an important new mission: helping the nation prepare for war.

The WPA and World War II

The possibility that the United States could be drawn into a major military conflict had grown stronger since the mid-1930s, as Nazi Germany, Japan, and Italy staged invasions or otherwise used their military power to gain control of new territory. Roosevelt had favored taking a strong stand against these nations as early as 1937. He argued in his so-called Quarantine Speech that the United States and its allies needed to contain these aggressors, though he did not explain the exact means by which that would be accomplished. Many Americans harbored strong isolationist sentiments, however, and the president's options were also restricted by a series of neutrality laws that Congress had enacted to prevent the United States from becoming involved in foreign conflicts.

Roosevelt's desire to increase American involvement in Europe received greater public support after Germany invaded Poland in September 1939, thus launching World War II. Though the United States would not officially enter the war until December 1941, the nation began providing supplies and armaments to Great Britain in 1939 and also began a large-scale buildup in its own defense capabilities. Shortly after Roosevelt secured a third term as president in November 1940, he declared that the United States "must be the great arsenal of democracy"[10] to oppose the Axis powers of Germany, Italy, and Japan. This perspective was increasingly shared by Congress and the American public, and war preparations accelerated further.

The WPA played an important part in these defense initiatives. Employment on the agency's Certified Defense and War Projects grew from 4 percent of WPA workers in July 1940 to 32 percent by December 1942. These projects encompassed a diverse range of tasks. The WPA's experience in airport con-

Women workers at a California factory that produced transparent plastic noses for bomber aircraft during World War II.

struction, for example, was utilized to build more than 200 military airfields and improve 160 others between 1940 and 1943. WPA workers also took on the task of building and improving roads that were deemed necessary for national defense.

In addition, large numbers of WPA workers were dispatched to military bases beginning in 1940. One of their main tasks was to build facilities to handle the influx of new military service members. This work became even more important after the nation's first peacetime draft began in October of that year. The agency's efforts extended beyond construction work, however. WPA health projects were launched at army and navy facilities, education and recreation programs were instituted specifically for military personnel, and WPA musicians were brought in to provide entertainment for the troops. Meanwhile, individuals from the WPA Art Program were put to work creating models, maps, and charts for training purposes. They even produced posters to highlight defense-related issues. The WPA Writers' Program made a similar turn to military projects.

As the entire nation moved toward a war footing, the WPA assisted private industry as it geared up for military production. Working in conjunction with the War Production Board and the U.S. Office of Education, the agency instituted special vocational training programs to prepare individuals for jobs building tanks, planes, ships, and countless other items needed by the armed forces. The 330,000 people who took part in these programs received a WPA security wage while they attended classes, then left the WPA rolls for a private industry job upon completing training. In some instances, participants received on-the-job instruction directly at factories that needed workers. These trainees also remained on the WPA payroll until they were hired as regular employees.

Women took part in these programs in large numbers to offset the growing number of men who joined the armed forces. By August 1942 more than 8,000 women were engaged in WPA vocational training. The agency also helped train aircraft mechanics, hospital workers, and others who took on war-related jobs.

A Farewell to Work Relief

The nation's involvement in World War II finally brought an end to the Great Depression. The federal government's massive wave of spending on military defense-related projects created a huge number of new jobs and revived the entire national economy. Between 1939 and 1941, unemployment in the United States dropped from nearly 9.5 million to just over 5.5 million, and the percentage of the work force without jobs fell below 10 percent for the first time since 1930. The economic resurgence hit high gear following the nation's official entrance into the war in late 1941. By 1943 the unemployment rate was just under 2 percent, a figure similar to that of the boom years of the 1920s.

As the unemployment rate dropped, so did the number of people employed by the WPA. At the end of 1939, the agency's work force stood at 2.1 million, but that figure dropped by half over the next two years. This decline was driven partly by the fact that fewer people needed a work-relief job and partly by steady reductions in the amount of money Congress allocated to the agency. The agency's work force dwindled even more quickly following the December 7,

1941, attack on Pearl Harbor that propelled the United States into direct engagement in World War II.

When the nation's unemployment problem vanished, the WPA became obsolete. On December 4, 1942, Roosevelt announced that the agency would soon cease operations (See "President Roosevelt Discontinues the WPA," p. 213). Employees wrapped up their assignments in the months that followed, and the WPA shut its doors for good on June 30, 1943, just over eight years after its creation. The end of the government's largest work-relief agency received only modest coverage in the press, and the WPA concluded its tasks with little of the fanfare, criticism, and debate that had characterized most of its existence. This quiet end did not diminish the importance of the government's grand experiment, however. The WPA had accomplished much during its life span, and its influence would extend far beyond the era of the Great Depression.

Notes

[1] Quoted in Gellerman, William. *Martin Dies.* New York: Da Capo, 1972, p. 68.

[2] Quoted in Watkins, T. H. *The Hungry Years: A Narrative History of the Great Depression in America.* New York: Holt, 1999, p. 255.

[3] Polenberg, Richard. *The Era of Franklin D. Roosevelt, 1933-1945: A Brief History with Documents.* Boston: Bedford/St. Martin's, 2000, p. 18.

[4] *Our Job with the WPA.* Washington, DC: U.S. Government Printing Office, n.d., p. 5.

[5] Taylor, p. 361.

[6] Taylor, p. 409.

[7] Quoted in McKinzie, Richard D. *The New Deal for Artists.* Princeton, NJ: Princeton University Press, 1973, p. 156.

[8] U.S. House of Representatives. *Report of the Special Committee on Un-American Activities Pursuant To H. Res. 282 (75th Congress).* 76th Cong., 1st sess., 1939. H. Rept. 2, p. 123.

[9] Quoted in McKinzie, p. 163.

[10] Roosevelt, Franklin D. *The Public Papers and Addresses of Franklin D. Roosevelt,* 1940 volume. New York: Macmillan, 1941, p. 643.

Chapter Seven

THE LEGACY OF THE WPA

⊰⊱

If private cooperative endeavor fails to provide work for willing hands and relief for the unfortunate, those suffering hardship through no fault of their own have a right to call on government for aid; and a government worthy of its name must make fitting response.[1]

—Franklin D. Roosevelt,
Annual Message to Congress, January 3, 1938

In creating the Works Progress Administration (WPA), the Roosevelt administration launched one of the boldest initiatives ever undertaken to address mass unemployment and relieve the hardship and hopelessness that accompany job loss. That initiative, combined with the other reforms and programs of the New Deal, stirred a heated debate that revolved around a central question: what role, if any, should the government play in helping those in need?

This question did not go away after the Great Depression ended. It has remained at the heart of many political deliberations in America, especially during periods of high unemployment and economic recession. When a prolonged economic recession took root in the United States and around the world in 2008, for example, the question returned with a vengeance. The history of the WPA, then, remains highly relevant to today's policymakers, economists, workers, and voters. Its legacy continues to be examined not only by people interested in U.S. history, but also by people seeking to address economic difficulties and social problems in the twenty-first century.

Combating Unemployment

In its eight years of operation, the WPA provided employment to 8.5 million Americans, far outpacing the other New Deal employment initiatives. The Civil Works Administration (CWA) added 4.2 million jobs and the Civilian Conservation Corps hired 2.75 million people. Many of the Americans who secured work through these agencies asserted that government employment saved them from ruin. "With my family," recalled one Oklahoman who lived through the Depression, "we would have starved to death [without government work programs]. Because we had no other way to make any money. The New Deal, [and] ... the WPA in particular, was just a lifesaver for us. Most of our neighbors felt that way."[2]

Even with its high volume of hiring, though, the WPA did not come anywhere close to providing a job to all of the Americans who needed one during the Great Depression. In Congressional testimony on the WPA, Harry Hopkins claimed that full employment was never the agency's goal. "The purpose of the Works Progress Administration is to provide useful work for particular groups of people in their particular skills. It [is] not our purpose to provide work for everybody."[3] Instead, the agency served as a bulwark to slow the flood of unemployment rather than stopping it completely. Judged on those terms, it was a success. But its effectiveness varied over time, depending on the funds it had available and the number of people needing help. At times, the WPA provided work for nearly 40 percent of the total Americans who had been unemployed, but that number also dropped as low as 17 percent during other periods of the Depression.[4]

The question remains whether work relief was the best option for helping suffering Americans during the Depression. The increased expense of a jobs program—as opposed to a program of direct relief—meant that fewer people could be assisted for each dollar spent. This was an important consideration when there were so many people needing help. The federal government's 1935 decision to end direct relief by replacing the Federal Emergency Relief Administration with the WPA also had unintended consequences. State and local governments became responsible for caring for anyone who was not on the WPA payroll, and many of those relief agencies had a very difficult time meeting their obligations because of their limited resources.

Despite these drawbacks, however, the WPA generally proved more acceptable than the dole in the minds of most Americans. It provided a way for government to offer aid while also allowing recipients to maintain a sense of use-fulness. The WPA also offered a form of assistance that upheld the value of work, which was extremely important in a country that was built on the ideal that talent and effort would be rewarded.

Improving Public and Military Infrastructure

The total price tag for the WPA's operations was $10.75 billion (roughly equivalent to $143 billion in 2012 dollars), an average of $1.3 billion ($17.3 billion in 2012 dollars) for each of the eight years it was in operation. This high expense was a particular point of criticism from people who thought that the rising federal deficit posed a major threat to America. But defenders of the WPA assert that the American people benefited enormously from these expenditures. WPA projects made lasting and notable improvements to the nation's public infrastructure, thus benefiting future generations of Americans. The federal con-struction projects that made up the bulk of the agency's efforts were indis-pensable in helping all areas of the country to upgrade roads, schools, gov-ernment buildings, parks, and numerous other facilities. These improvements were well beyond the financial reach of cash-strapped municipalities and states. Many of these works remain in use today, more than seventy years after they were built.

Some WPA critics have argued that these same infrastructure improve-ments could have been achieved at a lower cost had the government hired pri-vate contractors to complete the work instead of creating a government-run jobs program. WPA advocates claim, though, that infrastructure development using only private companies would have taken longer to implement and would not have provided the same level of help to the unemployed (since companies already had a work force in place). Private contractors would also have employed far fewer people in order to reduce their labor expenses—and thus increase their profits on projects.

As the nation prepared for World War II, the WPA became deeply involved in defense-related work. As the *Army and Navy Register* pointed out, "In the years 1935 to 1939, when regular appropriations for the armed forces were so meager, it was the WPA worker who saved many army posts and naval stations from literal obsolescence."[5] In addition, the agency's training programs played an important part in providing U.S. companies with skilled workers (both male and female) as war production increased.

Main entrance to Timberline Lodge, on Mount Hood in Oregon, which was built by the WPA in the 1930s.

Defenders of the WPA also say that the agency had a value that could never be calculated in terms of dollars and cents. They insist that the agency helped preserve the morale and skills of formerly unemployed citizens at a time when many of them were struggling with feelings of extreme desperation and hopelessness. The WPA performed a similar service for the country as a whole, helping it to maintain self-confidence and determination. "The Roosevelt administration placed an extraordinary bet on ordinary people, and the nation realized a remarkable return," wrote historian Nick Taylor. "The story of the WPA reminds us that the backbone of the United States is the strength, the patience and the underlying wisdom of its people when they are called upon to face a crisis and are given the means to overcome it."[6]

Work Relief as Economic Stimulus

For all of the achievements realized by the WPA and other New Deal work-relief programs, they did not bring about a full economic recovery. Supporters of federal work-relief programs and investments in new infrastructure asserted that they would revive the national economy and return it to health. This approach is sometimes known as Keynesian economics because it is based on theories championed by English economist John Maynard Keynes.

Plentiful evidence exists that government job creation and infrastructure investment did have a positive effect on the economy between 1933 and 1937. The impact of these economic stimulus programs became clear in 1937, when Roosevelt's decision to *cut* spending on the WPA and other New Deal programs triggered a sudden economic downturn. Even so, the Depression continued for more than five years after the WPA was created. The United States did not fully recover from the Great Depression until it began spending massive amounts of money for military purposes during World War II. Some historians and economists have thus concluded that the WPA and other New Deal stimulus programs were simply not large enough to overcome the Depression.

Another school of thought, which has been put forth by a number of conservative economists and historians, holds that the WPA and other New Deal initiatives were responsible for *prolonging* the Depression. They contend that the programs and policies launched by the Roosevelt administration created undue burdens on the business community through increased taxes and restrictions, which hampered job creation.

Supporters of this view generally believe that the better approach would have been to cut federal spending, reduce taxes, and eliminate tariffs to promote trade—in essence, to reduce the role of government in the economy. Whether such action would have ended the Depression sooner is a matter of debate, but the course of events in the early 1930s suggests that had Roosevelt taken this position, it would have been difficult for him in political terms. The 1932 presidential election clearly showed that a majority of American citizens wanted forceful action from their government to combat the Depression. They elected Roosevelt because he promised to "try something." A policy of cutting taxes, which would have given the government less revenue to provide assistance to unemployed workers and impoverished families, would likely have been very poorly received at a time when so many Americans were suffering.

Furthering the Reforms of the New Deal

Looking beyond the immediate implications of the Depression, the WPA played an important role in carrying forth New Deal reforms that have had a last-

A WPA vocational education class for African-American residents of New Orleans in 1936.

ing influence on American society and politics. "The New Deal instilled in Americans an unshakeable faith that their government stands ready to succor them in times of need," noted historian Michael Hiltzik. "Put another way, the New Deal established the concept of economic security as a collective responsibility."[7]

The WPA, more than any other New Deal program, applied this approach directly to the root problem of the Great Depression—mass unemployment. In so doing, it demonstrated that the government could not only provide financial support for destitute citizens but also give them job and vocational training opportunities that contributed to the wider public good. President Roosevelt's insistence on merging work with relief became one of the defining features of the New Deal, and he did not waver in his belief that a government-funded jobs program offered the best means for assisting the unemployed. This effort deeply touched many people. As one historian noted, "many working-men … who felt themselves to have been neglected in the past regarded Roosevelt as their friend. They sensed that … the president cared about what happened to them."[8]

This appreciation carried the president to four election victories, and it helped create a groundswell of support for progressive initiatives that endured long after the Depression was over. New Deal innovations such as Social Security for the elderly, unemployment insurance, Aid to Families with Dependent Children, and food stamps were expanded in the following decades, and they remain integral to the so-called social safety net that exists in the nation today.

In addition, major new expansions to the safety net have been enacted since the 1950s, including the Medicare and Medicaid health insurance programs established in the 1960s and the Patient Protection and Affordable Care Act of 2010, commonly known as Obamacare. With the adoption of these and other measures, the United States has developed a social system that gives the federal government much greater responsibility for the health and welfare of its citizens than it had before the Great Depression. Americans of different political persuasions are bitterly divided over whether these changes have benefited or injured the nation as a whole.

The government programs of the New Deal also made inroads in addressing social inequality and institutional racism in the United States. The WPA contributed to this civil rights effort by including large numbers of African Americans in its work projects and in the assistance programs of the National Youth Administration. The widespread involvement of blacks in work relief also persuaded many African Americans to switch their political allegiance to Roosevelt's Democratic Party. This migration set the stage for African Americans to emerge as an important segment of the Democratic coalition of voters.

The WPA's record in extending aid to women was less impressive, largely because the agency emphasized construction projects that used only male workers. Even so, the agency did help to bring women into wartime industries. Their strong work presence in these factories accelerated American society's acceptance of women in traditionally male-dominated workplaces. The percentage of women working outside the home grew steadily in the decades that followed.

The WPA also influenced attitudes about government support for arts and entertainment. Congress rebuffed calls to transform the Federal One programs

Poster for the 2009 National Book Festival, sponsored in part by the National Endowment for the Arts.

into a permanent government agency in the late 1930s, but the idea was revived in the 1960s. In 1965 President Lyndon Johnson signed legislation that created the National Endowment for the Arts (NEA), which remains the federal government's primary method for providing financial support for creative art. While the NEA owes a debt to the earlier WPA arts programs, its main function is to issue financial grants rather than to serve as a jobs program for artists. This design has allowed the endowment to remove itself from some of the controversial decisions about which artistic endeavors receive funding. However, the use of tax money to support creative work remains a political flash point. Many conservative Republicans strongly oppose the NEA, arguing that it promotes a liberal cultural and political agenda. Their criticisms frequently echo the complaints that opponents leveled against the Federal One arts programs during the Depression.

For many conservatives, though, government-funded art is just a symptom of a much larger problem. They view the increased presence of government in the daily existence of Americans as a problem rather than an achievement. These critics view the WPA and most other New Deal programs and policies in a negative light because they ushered in an era in which the U.S. government exerts more influence over business and personal affairs. They also assert that the current range of financial benefits offered by the U.S. government are too costly and need to be scaled back to reduce budget deficits.

Work Relief Programs since the Great Depression

While the WPA and other jobs programs formed an instrumental part of the New Deal, work relief did not become a permanent feature of the nation's social safety net. Some limited government-sponsored employment efforts have been undertaken since the Depression, but most have been relatively short-lived, and none have approached the scale of the WPA. This turn of events would not have pleased the New Deal's most ardent supporters of work relief. Harry Hopkins, for instance, argued that a permanent government work program should be included in the Social Security Act of 1935. This controversial proposal was abandoned, though, in order to gain additional congressional support for the Act from undecided legislators.

When President Roosevelt announced the end of the WPA in December 1942, he spoke of the desirability of establishing "a well-rounded public works program for the post-war period."[9] The National Resources Planning Board, a

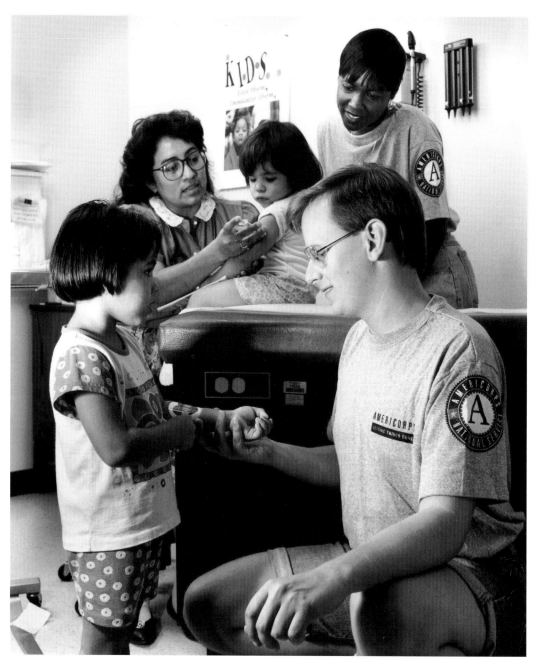

Americorps members provide a wide range of services, including health care services, to communities across the United States.

group responsible for assessing and planning federal public-works initiatives, proposed a similar idea that same year. U.S. leaders did not act upon these recommendations in the years that followed, however. It was not until the 1960s, during the administrations of Democratic presidents John F. Kennedy and Lyndon B. Johnson, that government-sponsored work and training programs were re-established. Many of these efforts were aimed at offering work, training, and education to young people from low-income families, with the Neighborhood Youth Corps being one such example.

Federal involvement in jobs programs expanded further in 1973 with the passage of the Comprehensive Employment and Training Act (CETA). Under CETA, as many as 742,000 people were employed at one time. Even at its peak, however, this initiative was far less expansive than the WPA. Employment was confined to service-sector jobs, and at its high point CETA provided work to only about 12 percent of the nation's unemployed citizens.[10] Not surprisingly, conservative critics attacked this endeavor as a poorly run exercise in make-work, and a fair amount of evidence existed to support that view. The various CETA-related programs were brought to a close in the early 1980s during the administration of Republican president Ronald Reagan, and work relief largely faded into the political shadows in the following decades.

As of 2012 the federal government maintained only a handful of small jobs programs. Founded in 1993, Americorps employs about 80,000 people a year to tutor disadvantaged youth, provide health care services, build affordable housing, run after-school programs, protect and conserve natural areas, and provide other services to needy communities across the United States. Americorps members perform this work in conjunction with nonprofit groups across the United States. The Peace Corps, which was founded in 1961, employs around 9,000 people annually to help communities in foreign lands with infrastructure development, health care, and education programs. In addition, the Federal Work Study (FWS) program provides jobs for low-income students attending college and other post-secondary institutions. This initiative has been functioning since 1964 and is in many ways similar to the Student Aid Program of the National Youth Administration.

Finally, the United States maintains various welfare-to-work or "workfare" programs that are designed to move recipients of public assistance into private employment. Enrollees in these programs are required to gain job experience, attend classes or training, or complete job-search activities in return for financial help. Many of these initiatives are related to the Temporary Assistance for Needy Families (TANF) program (the successor to Aid to Families with Dependent Children). TANF is funded by the federal government but implemented at the state level. As a result, welfare-to-work policies can vary greatly from state to state. Those programs that come the closest to providing a form of work relief place a strong emphasis on mandatory employment. In such cases, an individual receiving TANF payments is required to perform a certain number of hours of work at an unpaid job—usually at a government agency or nonprofit organization.

The American Recovery and Reinvestment Act

The WPA has received renewed attention since 2008, when the United States plunged into one of its worst economic crises since the Great Depression. Like Franklin Roosevelt in 1933, Barack Obama was sworn in as president in 2009 at a time when the nation faced high levels of unemployment, a tottering banking system, and other severe economic problems. Many observers hoped that the new Obama administration would launch a New Deal-style effort to create jobs and revive the economy. Instead, Obama and fellow Democrats in Congress pushed a broad stimulus bill called the American Recovery and Reinvestment Act (ARRA).

The $840 billion ARRA stimulus package was passed into law in February 2009. It encompassed a mix of elements designed to improve economic conditions, including tax cuts, investments in transportation and other infrastructure, increased money for unemployment benefits and job training, and funding for education, health care, housing, and family services. What it did not include was a specific jobs program. Instead, the aspects of ARRA that most directly affected unemployed workers fell into two areas.

First, the legislation increased expenditures on "direct relief" assistance, including expanded unemployment insurance payments and housing assistance. Second, it provided money to build roads and other infrastructure. These infrastructure improvements, however, were handled in a matter similar to the Depression-era Public Works Administration. The federal government paid private contractors to complete the projects, and the contractors made all the decisions about hiring. Consequently, there was no sudden surge in hiring similar to the one that America experienced when the CWA or WPA were launched. The gains in employment that resulted from Obama's stimulus package were more gradual because ARRA projects consisted mostly of infrastructure improvements, which took time to get up and running.

Why was the federal response to the 2008 recession so different from the one presented by Roosevelt during the Great Depression? The answer to this question sheds light on whether a massive jobs program similar to the WPA could ever again be enacted in the United States. Perhaps the most important factor to consider is the severity of the respective economic crises. While the misery created by the recession of the late 2000s and early 2010s was pronounced, it did not shake the nation's foundation to the same degree as the Great Depression. Even though 15.7 million people were out of work when joblessness reached its peak in October 2009—nearly three million more than in the worst year of the Great Depression—the total population of the United States had more than doubled since the 1930s. As a result, the unemployment rate in late 2009 was 10.2 percent, less than half of the staggering 25 percent unemployment rate that existed in 1933. Another important factor was that the twenty-first-century United States maintained a much more substantial social safety net than it did in the 1930s. Unemployment insurance and other forms of assistance that were not available during the Depression helped to soften some of the hardship experienced by those who lost their jobs during the late 2000s recession.

A number of political and logistical factors also likely influenced the policy decisions of the Obama administration. When President Obama took office, the United States was already running a budget shortfall in the neighborhood of $1.4 trillion. Even though deficit spending has become a more common practice since the Depression, this was the largest shortfall in the nation's history up to that point. Obama confronted a growing movement led by conservative Republicans to reduce the deficit. If the president had included a large-scale jobs program in the stimulus bill, he would have added significantly to its price tag, worsened the deficit, and endangered its passage by Congress. Many analysts believe that this was the primary reason the Obama administration decided to forego a direct work-relief initiative (see "Comparing the American Recovery and Reinvestment Act of 2009 to the WPA," p. 215).

Dim Prospects for a Twenty-First Century WPA

Had Obama taken a different course and attempted to create a contemporary version of the WPA, the agency would have faced other problems as well. During the Depression, the WPA could draw from a large pool of unemployed people who were capable and willing to take on the manual labor that powered

President Barack Obama delivers remarks at the work site for a bridge in Virginia funded by the American Recovery and Reinvestment Act.

the agency's construction work. "It's a different world now," noted one historian. "The work force is more white collar now, and white-collar workers don't have the skills to build bridges."[11] Other changes affecting the construction work of today are the increased regulation of such projects and the greater likelihood that new initiatives will be challenged by lawsuits, both of which can greatly slow the building process. Of course, a contemporary jobs program could focus on tasks other than construction, just as the WPA service projects did. To do so, however, officials would need to create jobs related to information technology and other industries that did not even exist in the 1930s.

These factors, along with the overall history of work relief in the United States, suggest that it is rather unlikely that the federal government will ever establish another program like the WPA. Even though various forms of public assistance have become well established since the time of the Depression, there has been a reluctance to undertake efforts that directly involve the government in managing employment. This distaste stems from the nation's strong

116

allegiance to private enterprise and personal initiative and its aversion to government interference in matters of commerce. It took the monumental crisis of the Great Depression to change public thinking on these matters in the 1930s, and it would likely require an economic meltdown of similar magnitude to bring about another broad-based work-relief program.

On the other hand, the events of the Great Depression illustrated that the people of the United States place a high value on taking care of one another in a time of need. It also showed that they are willing to experiment with bold new ideas to meet the crisis at hand. If another economic catastrophe does one day threaten the nation's social fabric, many people believe that the Works Progress Administration stands as an example of the type of innovative government response that may allow the United States to weather the storm.

Notes

[1] Roosevelt, Franklin D. *The Public Papers and Addresses of Franklin D. Roosevelt,* 1938 volume. New York: Macmillan, 1941, p. 1.

[2] Hodges, Pauline. Quoted in *The Dust Bowl: A Film by Ken Burns,* PBS. Episode 2. 2012.

[3] Quoted in Brock, William R. *Welfare, Democracy, and the New Deal.* Cambridge, UK: Cambridge University Press, 1988, p. 270.

[4] *Security, Work, and Relief Policies: Report of the Committee on Long-Range Work and Relief Policies to the National Resources Planning Board.* Washington, DC: U.S. Government Printing Office, 1942, p. 235.

[5] Quoted in *Final Report on the WPA Program 1935-43.* Washington, DC: U.S. Government Printing Office, 1947, p. 85.

[6] Taylor, Nick. *American Made: The Enduring Legacy of the WPA: When FDR Put the Nation to Work.* New York: Bantam, 2008, p. 4.

[7] Hiltzik, Michael. *The New Deal: A Modern History.* New York: Free Press, 2011, p. 424.

[8] Leuchtenburg, William Edward. *The FDR Years: On Roosevelt and His Legacy.* New York: Columbia University Press, 1995, p. 221.

[9] Roosevelt, Franklin D. *The Public Papers and Addresses of Franklin D. Roosevelt,* 1942 volume. New York: Harper & Brothers, 1950, p. 506.

[10] Rose, Nancy E. *Put to Work: Relief Programs in the Great Depression.* New York: Monthly Review Press, 1994, pp. 117-18.

[11] Wasserman, Mark. Quoted in Golway, Terry. "W.P.A. Projects Left Their Stamp on the Region," *New York Times,* April 15, 2009. Retrieved from http://www.nytimes.com/2009/04/19/nyregion/long-island/19Rwpa.html?pagewanted=all&_r=0.

BIOGRAPHIES

Mary McLeod Bethune (1875-1955)
Educator, Civil Rights Leader, and Director of the NYA's Office of Negro Affairs

Mary McLeod was born on July 10, 1875, near Mayesville, South Carolina. She was the daughter of former slaves who had gained their freedom just a decade before her birth. She grew up on her family's small farm in the company of seventeen siblings. From an early age Mary took inspiration from her mother and grandmother, strong-willed individuals who were leaders in the local African-American community.

After proving herself a gifted student at a local mission school, Mary earned a scholarship to attend Scotia Seminary for Negro Girls in North Carolina. Run by an integrated faculty, the school stressed racial equality and provided Mary with a positive environment that proved whites and blacks could work together. She went on to study at Moody Bible Institute in Chicago, where she was the school's only African-American student. Mary then embarked on a career as an educator, initially teaching at black schools in Georgia and South Carolina. In 1898 she married Albertus Bethune, and the couple had one son before separating.

Educates Black Students

In 1899 Mary McLeod Bethune took a teaching job in Florida. Five years later she founded her own school for African-American students, the Daytona Normal and Industrial Institute in Daytona Beach, which was financed by donations from both black and white residents in the local area. Bethune began with just five students and handmade school supplies, but she built the school into a respected and influential institution that steadily expanded its enrollment and course offerings. By the early 1920s it had 300 pupils, and in 1923 it merged with another school to become Bethune-Cookman College.

Bethune's work as an educator focused on helping blacks attain greater social equality and economic opportunities. Toward that end, her school worked to prepare future black leaders, particularly female leaders, and also provided training in nursing and other vocations.

Bethune's crusading efforts to empower African Americans extended beyond the classroom as well. She organized a campaign to increase African-American voting in her community, for instance, which prompted a tense—though nonviolent—confrontation with the Ku Klux Klan. She also assumed a leadership role in the women's club movement, which served as a powerful force in organizing black political power. In the mid-1920s she became the president of the National Association of Colored Women.

Joins the New Deal

Bethune's expertise in education and her involvement in public affairs brought her into contact with prominent political leaders of both parties. Up until the Great Depression, she—like many other African Americans—supported the Republican Party, which had worked to abolish slavery and establish equal rights for black citizens during and after the Civil War. When Democrat Franklin D. Roosevelt (FDR) became president in 1933, however, Bethune became a supporter of the president's New Deal economic stimulus policies. Her connection to the administration was further strengthened by her friendship with Eleanor Roosevelt. In 1935 Bethune was appointed to the advisory committee for the National Youth Administration (NYA) of the Works Progress Administration (WPA). A year later, FDR chose her to head the newly created NYA Office of Negro Affairs.

The skills that Bethune had honed in her previous work served her well in her new post, and she was extremely effective in winning support for initiatives to assist African-American youth. Under her guidance, in fact, the NYA built one of the best records among the New Deal programs in regard to offering black citizens their fair share of benefits. Of the more than 300,000 African Americans who took part in the program, 180,000 were high school students who were able to continue their studies thanks to the NYA Student Aid Program. In addition, Bethune was a driving force behind the creation of the Special Negro Higher Education Fund for black college students.

On another front, Bethune successfully lobbied the president to create residential training camps for African Americans. These facilities provided young women with instruction in areas such as food preparation and laundry work and taught young men skills related to farming, construction, automotive repair, and machine-shop operations.

The camps, however, were constrained by the racial bigotry of the era. The facilities were segregated by race, and training options for blacks were largely confined to manual-labor jobs that African Americans had typically filled in the past. In Bethune's view, however, the NYA programs offered practical assistance to individuals during a particularly difficult economic period and provided greater—though not ideal—opportunities to black Americans. "If the children of the Negro people must adjust themselves to the White man's civilization," she wrote, "[and] fit themselves into the White man's industrial scheme, ... then they must have an equal measure with the White man's children in thoroughness of preparation."[1]

Becomes a Civil Rights Pioneer

Bethune also used her position in the Roosevelt administration to further the broader crusade for racial equality. One of her highest priorities was to place African Americans in positions of authority within the NYA. She believed that this process would not only allow the agency to better serve blacks but would also open the door to additional minority hiring in the federal government and help create the next generation of black leaders. By 1939 she had succeeded in placing twenty-five African Americans, including six women, in administrative positions in various state offices of the agency.

Bethune understood the importance of building a broad-based movement to bring about social change. Toward this end, she was instrumental in forming the Federal Council of Negro Affairs in 1936. Better known as the "Black Cabinet," this group consisted of African Americans who were employed in positions of authority throughout the federal government. Bethune called the group together for weekly meetings at her home, where they discussed issues of importance to the nation's black citizens and ways to coordinate their actions to achieve progress in the civil rights struggle. On another front, she consulted with Democratic officials on electoral matters and pressed them to take further action on racial issues.

Bethune and the other black members of the Roosevelt administration suffered defeats as well as victories. One of their biggest disappointments was their inability to convince President Roosevelt to support anti-lynching legislation. They did make civil rights a more prominent topic of political dialogue, however, which helped set the stage for the advances that would take place in the 1950s and 1960s.

Bethune remained with the NYA until it ceased operation in 1943. Later that year she was forced to fend off attacks by the House Un-American Activities Committee (HUAC) after it tried to brand her a communist. She successfully refuted the charge, though, and emerged from the experience as an outspoken critic of HUAC and other anticommunist investigations. After leaving the NYA, Bethune focused on her work as president of the National Council of Negro Women, a government lobbying group she had formed in 1935. In her later years, she received widespread acclaim and numerous honorary degrees for her pioneering work in education, government service, and civil rights. Bethune died of a heart attack at her home in Daytona Beach on May 18, 1955, at the age of seventy-nine.

Sources

Botsch, Carol Sears. "Mary McLeod Bethune." n.d. University of South Carolina—Aiken. Retrieved from http://www.usca.edu/aasc/bethune.htm.

Hanson, Joyce A. *Mary McLeod Bethune and Black Women's Political Activism.* Columbia: University of Missouri Press, 2003.

McClusky, Audrey Thomas, and Elaine M. Smith. *Mary McLeod Bethune: Building a Better World, Essays and Selected Documents.* Bloomington: Indiana University Press, 1999.

Note

[1] Quoted in Hanson, Joyce A. *Mary McLeod Bethune and Black Women's Political Activism.* Columbia: University of Missouri Press, 2003, p. 145.

Martin Dies Jr. (1900-1972)
*Conservative Congressman and Chair of the
House Un-American Activities Committee
(HUAC)*

Martin Dies Jr. was born on November 5, 1900, in Colorado City, Texas. As an infant he moved with his parents to the city of Beaumont, and East Texas remained his home for the rest of his life. His views and his later career in politics were strongly influenced by his father, Martin Dies Sr., a lawyer and politician who served as a member of the U.S. Congress from 1909 to 1919.

The younger Dies attained his law degree at National University in Washington, D.C., in 1920. He married the former Myrtle Adams the same year, and the marriage eventually produced three sons. Dies practiced law at his father's law firm in Orange, Texas, during the 1920s before opting to enter politics. In November 1930 he was elected to the same seat that his father had once held in the U.S. House of Representatives. The thirty-year-old Democrat was the youngest member of Congress when he took office.

A Conservative Legislator

Dies began his legislative career as the Great Depression was tightening its grip on the nation. He initially supported strong federal action to revive the economy and create jobs. During his first years in Washington, he railed against what he called "the giants of concentrated wealth"[1] and urged his colleagues to impose stronger regulations on large corporations. He also collaborated on a plan that called for increased spending on public works as a means of boosting employment, but President Herbert Hoover ignored this proposal.

After fellow Democrat Franklin D. Roosevelt took office in 1932, Dies was among the lawmakers who backed the early legislative measures of the New Deal, which focused on business regulation, unemployment relief, and agricultural reform. Even as late as 1936, Dies expressed admiration for the president, stating that "no man has ever demonstrated more completely his independence and honesty than Franklin D. Roosevelt."[2]

125

On other matters, however, Dies staunchly opposed the liberal measures promoted by the Roosevelt administration. Dies strongly believed in the concept of individual liberty, particularly in economic matters. The congressman worried that this ideal was being imperiled as the federal government took on more power and played a larger role in citizens' daily lives. Also, like many Southern politicians, he was a strong proponent of states' rights and did not want the federal government to interfere with the region's system of racial segregation.

Dies also became one of Washington, D.C.'s most outspoken critics of the nation's immigration policies. Convinced that the nation's unemployment problem was caused mainly by the large number of people from other countries who had settled in the United States, he repeatedly sponsored bills calling for a moratorium on legal immigration and the deportation of individuals who had entered the country illegally. To garner public support for his position, he claimed that many of the non-citizens living in the country were communists sent by the Soviet Union who planned to seize control of the government through an "armed uprising."[3]

Staunch Anti-communist and New Deal Opponent

As the Roosevelt administration rolled out the liberal policies known collectively as the Second New Deal, Dies turned decisively against the president. He denounced Roosevelt's court-packing plan and criticized the president's support for the sit-down strike at General Motors in Flint, Michigan, which Dies believed was orchestrated by communists. By the close of 1937 Dies had formally allied himself with a growing anti-New Deal coalition of Republicans and conservative Democrats.

Around the same time, Dies grew more emphatic in his warnings about the danger of communism. In June 1938 he succeeded in his quest to establish the House Un-American Activities Committee (HUAC) and was appointed as its chair. Under Dies's leadership, HUAC conducted controversial investigations of alleged communist activity in the United States.

Dies and his fellow committee members aired numerous charges against government employees, business leaders, celebrities, and ordinary citizens in a series of intense, high-profile hearings. Instead of considering such charges in a thorough, unbiased manner, however, HUAC relied heavily on hearsay evidence and guilt by association. If a witness testified that he saw a Federal Theatre Project (FTP) employee in possession of a communist newspaper, for instance, the committee accepted the allegation as evidence that the FTP was dominated by communists. If an individual was identified (rightly or wrongly) as a communist, other groups of which he or she was a member also were denounced as fronts for communist activity. HUAC even labeled groups like the Boy Scouts and the Camp Fire Girls as communistic on the basis of such "evidence."

Dies focused much of his attention on the WPA arts programs. He maintained that his committee had solid evidence of "Communist domination in WPA's Federal Writers and Federal Theatre Projects" and that "one-third of the Federal Writers Project were Communists."[4] Such charges raised concerns about leftist influence in the WPA and helped lay the groundwork for passage of the Emergency Relief Appropriation Act of 1939, which placed new constraints on WPA operations. Several of the reforms mandated by the law stemmed from Dies's investigations or reflected his philosophy. These provisions included the overhaul of the arts programs, the institution of a loyalty oath for WPA workers, and the exclusion of non-citizens from agency employment.

Fading Influence

Although the media attention surrounding the HUAC hearings in the 1930s and 1940s raised Dies's profile on the national level, he ultimately failed to advance his political career. In 1941 he was soundly defeated in a bid for a seat in the U.S. Senate. He continued to hold his House seat and his chairmanship of HUAC through the early 1940s, but he did not seek reelection in 1944 due to growing political opposition in his district.

After practicing law in Lufkin, Texas, for a time, Dies was once more elected to the House of Representatives in 1952. He served three terms before stepping down in 1959. He did not serve as a member of HUAC during this period. Instead, anti-communist crusaders such as Senator Joseph McCarthy, who had learned a great deal from Dies's tactics, stepped to the forefront on this issue. In his final campaign in 1957, Dies made a second unsuccessful bid to represent Texas in the Senate.

The degree to which Dies sincerely believed that the United States faced a widespread communist threat is a matter of considerable speculation. Some historians view him as an opportunist who used the HUAC investigations primarily to discredit Roosevelt and other liberals and to increase his own political stature. Historians who believe Dies's concerns were genuine, on the other hand, point out that his anti-communist rhetoric continued even after he left

127

office. "The Liberal front is picking up where the New Deal front left off," he warned in 1963, "and together they are pushing us toward Socialism and ultimate Communism."[5] Dies's political commentary appeared frequently in *American Opinion*, the official magazine of the archconservative John Birch Society, during the 1960s. He passed away in Lufkin on November 14, 1972, at the age of seventy-two.

Sources

Dies, Martin. *Martin Dies' Story*. New York: Bookmailer, 1963.

Gellermann, William. *Martin Dies*. 1944. Reprint, New York: Da Capo, 1972.

Green, George N. "Dies, Martin." Handbook of Texas Online. Texas State Historical Association. Retrieved from http://www.tshaonline.org/handbook/online/articles/fdi13.

Notes

[1] Quoted in Gellermann, William. *Martin Dies*. 1944. Reprint, New York: Da Capo, 1972, p. 33.

[2] Quoted in Gellerman, p. 53.

[3] Quoted in Gellerman, p. 47.

[4] Dies, Martin. *Martin Dies' Story*. New York: Bookmailer, 1963, p. 67.

[5] Dies, p. 205.

Harry Hopkins (1890-1946)
Director of the Works Progress Administration from 1935 to 1938

Harry Lloyd Hopkins was born on August 17, 1890, in Sioux City, Iowa. His family lived in several Midwestern towns during his youth before settling in Grinnell, Iowa. His mother was a serious, deeply religious woman who dedicated herself to helping those less fortunate. His father, on the other hand, was a boisterous man-about-town who gambled on bowling to boost the family income. Hopkins's character included elements inherited from both of his parents, but it was the influence of his mother and older sister that helped convince him to become a social worker.

As a student at Grinnell College, Hopkins became involved in the social gospel movement, which advocated for social reforms based on Christian principles. After graduating in 1912, he took a job at a settlement house in New York City that aided disadvantaged residents of the Lower East Side. The following year he married Ethel Gross. They became the parents of four children before the marriage ended in divorce in 1931. Hopkins and his second wife, Barbara Duncan, had one daughter before Barbara died in 1937. Five years later Hopkins married his third wife, Louise Macy.

Tireless Social Service Administrator

Skilled and ambitious, Hopkins landed a series of administrative positions with public and private aid organizations during the 1910s and 1920s. These jobs took him from New York to New Orleans, Louisiana, and Atlanta, Georgia. Hopkins soon gained a reputation for dispensing with red tape and attaining results, and he inspired his employees through the example of his own exhausting work habits. "He was intense," remembered a colleague, "seeming to be in a perpetual nervous ferment—a chain smoker and black coffee drinker."[1]

Hopkins balanced his go-getter personality with a deep empathy for the people he helped. Believing that the poor should be treated with dignity rather than disdain, he favored programs that allowed aid recipients to retain their independence and make their own decisions. Perhaps most importantly, he realized the essential role that work could play in helping people turn their lives around. One of his earliest experiments in work relief came in the mid-1910s, when he oversaw a program in New York that employed low-income residents in the city parks.

Master of Emergency Relief

With the arrival of the Great Depression in 1929, Hopkins put work relief into practice on a much wider basis. After initially running a private jobs program, he was appointed executive secretary of the New York Temporary Emergency Relief Administration (TERA) by Governor Franklin D. Roosevelt in 1931. TERA proved to be a pioneering agency in the area of work relief, giving jobs to more than one million of the state's residents while also distributing direct relief. Soon after Roosevelt was elected president in 1932, Hopkins began crafting a plan that adapted many aspects of TERA for use on the national level. His outline became the basis of the Federal Emergency Relief Administration (FERA). On May 22, 1933—his first day as the director of the new agency—Hopkins issued more than $5 million in grants to states that had applied for relief funding.

Hopkins wanted to get assistance to the destitute as quickly as possible, so the agencies he led distributed funds and jobs at a breakneck pace. He made no apologies about the expense involved and had little patience for complaints that he was careless with taxpayer money. In fact, Hopkins was a fierce defender of New Deal relief efforts. "They are damn good projects—excellent projects," he said in response to a question at a 1935 press conference about an allegedly wasteful work relief initiative. "You know, dumb people criticize something they do not understand, and that is what is going on up there—God damn it! Here are a lot of people broke and we are putting them to work."[2]

Hopkins's blunt manner and uncompromising views frequently vaulted him into the center of public debate over the New Deal. Conservative commentators criticized him for presiding over wasteful boondoggles and leading the country down the path to socialism. A *Chicago Daily Tribune* editorial from 1936, for instance, stated that "Mr. Hopkins is a bullheaded man whose high place in the New Deal was won by his ability to waste more money in quicker time on more absurd undertakings than any other mischievous wit in Washington could think of."[3]

Such attacks, however, had little effect on Hopkins's behavior or on his belief in his mission. "Without being flamboyant, he was kind of cocky," remembered one associate. "At the same time he was absolutely dedicated to the cause of the unemployed, and he was prepared to try anything that could be done to help poor people."[4]

Playing Politics

By the mid-1930s, Hopkins had become one of the most important figures in the Roosevelt administration. Fiercely loyal to the president and able to juggle numerous responsibilities efficiently, he increasingly became Roosevelt's go-to administrator. In mid-1935 the president selected Hopkins to guide the newly created Works Progress Administration (WPA), the largest work-relief enterprise of the entire New Deal era. During this same period, Hopkins played an important role in drafting the Social Security Act of 1935.

Hopkins spent a lot of his time working to secure political support for the president and his policies. In service to this goal, the director reluctantly cooperated with powerful political figures around the country who sometimes used WPA jobs to boost their own influence. "I thought at first I could be completely non-political," Hopkins once said. "Then they told me I had to be part non-political and part political. I found that was impossible, at least for me. I finally realized that there was nothing for it but to be all-political."[5]

As Hopkins increased his political activities, he began flirting with the idea of running for president in the 1940 election. Roosevelt, who initially intended to leave office at the end of his second term, encouraged this plan. For a time, Roosevelt seemed to favor Hopkins as his successor. The president even relieved Hopkins of his WPA responsibilities in late 1938 to make him his secretary of commerce. This move was interpreted as an effort by Roosevelt to give his friend and advisor broader government experience.

Hopkins's potential candidacy faced a number of challenges, however. For one thing, he was a politically divisive figure who had never held elected office. His health was another pressing concern. After undergoing surgery for stomach cancer in 1937, Hopkins became severely malnourished. By the summer of 1939 his condition had become so grave that he was forced to resign as secretary of commerce. A short time later, the outbreak of war in Europe helped convince Roosevelt to seek a third term, dealing a final blow to Hopkins's presidential aspirations.

"Deputy President"

Although the commerce department proved to be Hopkins's last official government stop, he continued to provide valuable service to Roosevelt. His health gradually improved with the assistance of naval doctors, and Hopkins became the president's most trusted advisor on issues related to World War II. Hopkins made frequent trips to Europe to meet with world leaders such as British prime minister Winston Churchill and Soviet premier Joseph Stalin. He also supervised the Lend-Lease program that provided armaments and supplies to those countries as they battled Nazi Germany. In addition, Hopkins turned his organizational skills to the task of preparing U.S. industrial and military forces for war. His prominent stature in the Roosevelt administration during these years caused many journalists to refer to him as the "deputy president." Hopkins even had the distinction of residing at the White House from 1940 to 1943.

Hopkins accomplished his wartime work in spite of his fragile medical condition, which in some cases reduced his working capacity to a few hours a day. By the time of the Yalta Conference, which took place in Russia in February 1945, he was too ill to attend many of the meetings. Nevertheless, Hopkins insisted on being on hand as Roosevelt, Stalin, and Churchill discussed Allied military strategy and the organization of postwar Europe. Hopkins was hospitalized upon his return to the United States, so he was unable to see Roosevelt again before the president died in April. In the months that followed, Hopkins assisted President Harry S. Truman in his efforts to negotiate a peace treaty to end World War II. Hopkins then returned to New York City, where he died on January 29, 1946, at the age of fifty-five.

Sources

Hopkins, June. *Harry Hopkins: Sudden Hero, Brash Reformer.* New York: St. Martin's, 1999.
McJimsey, George. *Harry Hopkins: Ally of the Poor and Defender of Democracy.* Cambridge, MA: Harvard University Press, 1987.
Sherwood, Robert E. *Roosevelt and Hopkins: An Intimate History.* New York: Harper, 1950.

Notes

[1] Quoted in Sherwood, Robert E. *Roosevelt and Hopkins: An Intimate History.* New York: Harper, 1950, p. 29.
[2] Quoted in Sherwood, p. 60.
[3] "Human Needs and Washington Politicians." *Chicago Daily Tribune,* April 17, 1936, p. 14.
[4] Quoted in Louchheim, Katie, ed. *The Making of the New Deal: The Insiders Speak.* Cambridge, MA: Harvard University Press, 1983, p. 190.
[5] Quoted in Sherwood, p. 68.

Lyndon B. Johnson (1908-1973)
Texas Director of the WPA's National Youth Administration and President of the United States from 1963 to 1969

Lyndon Baines Johnson (often referred to by his initials, LBJ) was born in the tiny community of Stonewall in the Texas Hill Country on August 27, 1908. His parents both hailed from prominent local families, and his father and maternal grandfather served in the Texas House of Representatives. His family, however, struggled with financial setbacks due to his father's unsuccessful speculation in cotton.

Johnson attended Southwest Texas State Teachers College. While completing his studies, he worked as a teacher and principal in a Hispanic school in South Texas, where he got a first-hand look at extreme poverty. After earning his degree in 1930, Johnson worked briefly as a high school teacher. The following year he moved to Washington, D.C., to serve as an assistant to a Texas congressional representative.

When Democrat Franklin D. Roosevelt was elected president in 1932, during the depths of the Great Depression, Johnson viewed him as a hero and role model. He became an ardent supporter of the president's New Deal programs, which were designed to create jobs, stimulate the economy, and provide assistance to struggling Americans. Johnson knew that the Great Depression had left many of the residents of the Texas Hill Country facing utter destitution, and he felt a genuine desire to help them. As an aspiring politician, though, he also realized that the sweeping changes brought about by the New Deal could bring opportunities to advance his own career.

Directs the Texas NYA

As part of the Works Progress Administration initiative, Roosevelt created the National Youth Administration (NYA) to assist young people. The new agency needed a director for each state. In 1935 Johnson used his connections with influential legislators to secure an appointment as director of the Texas NYA. At twenty-six years old, he was the youngest state director in the country.

What he may have lacked in experience, though, Johnson made up for in dedication. He routinely worked sixteen hours a day, seven days a week, and drove his staff equally hard. "Everything had to be done NOW," remembered one of his employees. "And he could get very, very angry if something couldn't be done immediately."[1] Despite his demanding personality, Johnson was an effective leader who had a knack for inspiring people to complete the challenging tasks he handed them. Among those he called upon to aid the mission was Claudia Alta "Lady Bird" Johnson, whom he had married the year before.

Johnson managed to clear bureaucratic roadblocks to get the NYA student assistance program off to a fast start. Within a year, 11,000 high school students and nearly 5,500 college students in Texas had received jobs. One of Johnson's most innovative ideas came in the agency's work-relief program for non-students: he put young people to work building motorist rest stops along the state's highways. This initiative proved to be so successful that numerous other states undertook similar programs. Johnson also championed the creation of "Freshman Centers" that offered college classes to individuals who were unable to travel to more distant campuses. This novel idea inspired the creation of the nation's community college system.

A particularly challenging aspect of Johnson's job involved finding ways to assist minorities. NYA leaders at the national level urged state directors to reach out to African Americans, but this was a politically risky undertaking for Johnson. Texas observed a strict policy of racial segregation at that time. Johnson's solution was to provide assistance to minorities in ways that would draw little public attention. He quietly dispensed a large amount of aid to black students and workers and established educational and vocational centers to serve African Americans and Hispanics.

Meanwhile, Johnson avoided taking stronger actions that might stir up white resistance. He refused to appoint African-American staff and board members as requested by the national NYA leadership, and he kept all of the agency's programs segregated. Despite its limitations, Johnson's pragmatic approach had a very positive impact in the African-American community. His performance pleased black leaders such as the NYA's Mary McLeod Bethune. It also impressed an NYA regional director who described Johnson as "easily one of the best men directing one of the best staffs in one of the best programs with the most universal and enthusiastic public support of any state in the Union."[2]

Congressional Powerbroker and Vice President

Throughout his time with the NYA, Johnson viewed the position as a stepping stone to public office. When a Texas congressional representative passed away in 1937, Johnson jumped into the race to fill the vacant seat. In April of that year, at the age of twenty-eight, he was elected to the U.S. House of Representatives. The leadership skills and hard-driving work habits that he had developed with the youth agency proved equally valuable in Congress, and Johnson quickly became known as a shrewd politician with valuable connections to Roosevelt and other influential leaders. He loyally backed the president's policies until FDR's death in 1945. In the late 1940s and into the 1950s, however, Johnson adopted a more conservative stance—particularly on civil rights and labor issues.

Eager to advance his career, Johnson won election to the U.S. Senate in 1948, following an earlier unsuccessful attempt to join the upper chamber. As a senator, he demonstrated exceptional skill as a dealmaker. Johnson became famous for his ability to foster compromise, cajole his colleagues, and "twist the arms" of reluctant legislators when necessary. These skills made him one of the most important members of Congress, especially after he was elected senate majority leader in 1956.

Four years later, Johnson launched a presidential campaign. Although he lost the Democratic nomination to Massachusetts senator John F. Kennedy, Kennedy selected Johnson as his vice presidential running mate in hopes of bolstering his popularity in the South. After the Kennedy-Johnson ticket won the 1960 election and took office, however, the Texan was given little opportunity to contribute to the administration's political or legislative efforts. For a time, Johnson worried that the vice presidency represented a dead end in his political career. But everything changed on November 22, 1963, when Kennedy was killed by an assassin's bullet. A few hours later, Johnson was sworn in as the thirty-sixth president of the United States.

Revives the Spirit of the New Deal

During his time in the White House, Johnson once again embraced his earlier role as a political progressive. He threw his support behind the civil rights movement, for instance, guiding Kennedy's Civil Rights Act of 1964 through Congress and securing passage of the Voting Rights Act of 1965. Johnson also redefined the role of the federal government in providing aid to poor and elderly Americans. He signed the legislation that established the Medicare and Medicaid public health insurance programs, for example, and he enacted a series of education and antipoverty reforms with his Great Society initiative.

Johnson's Great Society programs reminded many observers of Roosevelt's New Deal. Johnson acknowledged the influence in a planning meeting for the Economic Opportunity Act of 1964 (EOA), when he proudly stated that "I'm an old NYA man."[3] Under his leadership, the Great Society initiative included employment and vocational-training programs similar to those he oversaw in the 1930s, such as the Neighborhood Youth Corps, the Job Corps, and the Federal Work-Study Program.

Even as he was finding success with his domestic policy agenda, however, Johnson's presidency crumbled because of the Vietnam War. American involvement in the messy civil war in Vietnam had steadily escalated throughout 1964, and in 1965 Johnson began sending large numbers of U.S. troops into the war. When the conflict hardened into a bloody stalemate, Johnson came under intense criticism. With bitter debate over Vietnam dividing the nation and casting a dark shadow over his presidency, Johnson chose not to seek reelection in 1968. He returned home to Texas after leaving office in January 1969. At that point Johnson's health steadily declined due to heart disease. He died of a heart attack on January 22, 1973, at the age of sixty-four.

Sources

Caro, Robert A. *The Years of Lyndon Johnson: The Path to Power.* New York: Knopf, 1982.

Dallek, Robert. *Lone Star Rising: Lyndon Johnson and His Times, 1908-1960.* New York: Oxford University Press, 1991.

Notes

[1] Quoted in Dallek, Robert. *Lone Star Rising: Lyndon Johnson and His Times, 1908-1960.* New York: Oxford University Press, 1991, p. 130.

[2] Quoted in Dallek, p. 143.

[3] Quoted in McKee, Guian A. "Lyndon B. Johnson and the War on Poverty." Presidential Recordings of Lyndon B. Johnson. Retrieved from http://presidentialrecordings.rotunda.upress.virginia.edu.

Mr. Mahoney (1883-?)
Works Progress Administration Employee during the Great Depression

M r. Mahoney was one of the 8.5 million people in the United States who found employment with the Works Progress Administration (WPA). His experience was chronicled in a study of relief recipients conducted in 1940 by the Columbia University Council for Research in the Social Sciences. Though the name "Mahoney" is a pseudonym, all details in the case study pertain to an actual person (whose first name is not provided). His story offers insight into the experiences of the general laborers who joined the WPA workforce.

From Work to the Dole

Born in Northern Ireland in 1883, Mr. Mahoney grew up on a small farm. After completing his grammar (elementary) school studies, he moved to a near-by city to work as a construction helper. He later became a cement mason. While in his thirties, Mahoney met his future wife, an Irish native who had pre-viously worked in the United States. Believing there was greater opportunity in America, they immigrated in 1921. Mahoney found a job helping to build sub-way lines in New York City.

The couple married in 1925, and their daughter, Cecilia, was born three years later. During the prosperous years of the late 1920s, Mahoney's employ-ment remained fairly steady, and he usually brought home around $130 a month (about $1,800 in 2012 dollars). He told the researchers conducting the study that "he never had to count his pennies and always had money in his pocket"[1] during that time.

The Mahoneys did not accumulate much savings, however, so they found themselves in difficult financial circumstances when the U.S. economy entered the severe downturn known as the Great Depression. Mr. Mahoney's work opportunities dwindled and the family was forced to share an apartment with Mrs. Mahoney's sister to save money. Finally, in August 1933, his work gave out completely. He was unable to find other employment, and by November their rent and utility bills were months overdue. With no other options avail-able, the Mahoney family applied for relief assistance. Though Mr. Mahoney requested that he be placed in a work relief job, the family was assigned to home (direct) relief instead. The Mahoneys thus joined millions of other Americans "on the dole."

The family later reported that "they do not even like to think about the trouble they had managing on Home Relief."[2] Although the rent on their apartment exceeded the housing allowance they received, Mahoney and his wife were unable to locate cheaper accommodations. As a result, they were forced to use some of their food money to pay the rent. This, in turn, meant that they did not have enough to eat. The lack of proper nutrition may have contributed to the frequent illnesses suffered by five-year-old Cecilia. Mr. Mahoney spent most of his time traveling throughout the city in a fruitless search for work.

WPA Construction Worker

After nearly a year on the dole, Mr. Mahoney learned in October 1934 that he had been approved for a work relief assignment paying $61.40 per month. Though the details are unclear, he was likely employed through more than one jobs program in the months that followed. After the WPA began operation in 1935, he went to work for that agency.

As a trained cement mason, Mahoney was well suited to the construction work that was the principal focus of the WPA, and he was able to continue practicing his primary trade throughout his years with the agency. He reported that the jobs he worked on were fairly well managed and that the quality of the work completed was similar to that in private industry. He also noted, though, that poor planning by administrators and insufficient funding of the program sometimes caused difficulties for the workers.

In terms of money, Mahoney's WPA job represented a significant improvement over direct relief. Because he was classified as a skilled laborer, his pay was relatively high for a WPA worker ($82 to $85 per month). This sum enabled the family to rent a three-room apartment in the Washington Heights section of Manhattan. They also managed to pay off their debts and buy reasonable levels of groceries.

The work relief wages were still only about two-thirds of what Mahoney had made at his private-industry jobs, however, so the family maintained a frugal lifestyle. There was little money available to spend on clothing, household goods, or entertainment. They also endured more severe financial problems on those occasions when Mr. Mahoney's work hours were reduced due to bad weather.

The family's fragile economic fortunes took a severe hit in the late summer of 1939. Mr. Mahoney was forced to give up his WPA job after Congress mandated that workers could not be employed with the agency for more than eighteen months at a time. The family returned to direct relief for six weeks. At that point, however, Mr. Mahoney managed to gain re-entry onto the WPA payroll. His return to the WPA greatly lifted the spirits of the Mahoney household.

Overall, the Mahoneys found work relief to be much preferable to the dole. "They realize that WPA is a kind of Relief," the interviewer noted, "but since Mr. Mahoney gives some return for the relief given them he is able to keep up his self-respect."[3] The couple also appreciated the fact that the program allowed them to make their own decisions on how to spend their money. Finally, Mr. Mahoney was especially glad that he was able to continue working, because he believed that "one of the worst things that can happen to a man is to lose his skills and get 'soft' because then there is little chance for reemployment."[4]

Optimism about the Future

The interviewers had no further contact with the Mahoneys after the beginning of 1940, so it is uncertain what became of the family. Their observations, however, offer hints of their possible future. At the time the study was conducted, Mr. Mahoney was worried that his WPA work could suddenly come to an end. His fear may have come to pass, given the general reduction in work relief that took place in the early 1940s. He also realized that, at age fifty-seven, "he is pretty old and he knows that old men are not being hired"[5] by many private employers.

Despite these uncertainties, Mr. Mahoney remained optimistic and believed that he would be able to find work if the Depression came to an end. Given that the economy did rebound strongly as the country prepared for and then entered World War II, it is possible that he was able to move into a private-industry construction job at some point in the early 1940s. In addition, the prospect of war opened up other employment opportunities, so he may have found work in one of the defense-related industries. At the time of the interview, he had already put in an application at the Brooklyn Navy Yard, which at the height of the war expanded its work force to 75,000 employees.

Whatever the future held for the Mahoneys, they viewed the WPA as a helpful but temporary program to get Americans through hard times. "They do not feel that WPA is the answer to the unemployment problem," the interviewer noted. "The only answer, as they see it, is … the opening up of private employment."[6]

Sources

Ginzberg, Eli. *The Unemployed.* Edited by Ben B. Seligman. New Brunswick, NJ: Transaction, 2004.

Taylor, Nick. *American-Made: The Enduring Legacy of the WPA, When FDR Put the Nation to Work.* New York: Random House, 2009.

Notes

[1] Quoted in Ginzberg, Eli. *The Unemployed.* Edited by Ben B. Seligman. New Brunswick, NJ: Transaction, 2004, p. 276.

[2] Quoted in Ginzberg, p. 273.

[3] Quoted in Ginzberg, p. 274.

[4] Quoted in Ginzberg, p. 271.

[5] Quoted in Ginzberg, p. 276.

[6] Quoted in Ginzberg, p. 273.

Jackson Pollock (1912-1956)
Painter and Member of the WPA Federal Art Project

Paul Jackson Pollock was born on January 29, 1912, in Cody, Wyoming. His family moved numerous times during his childhood, as his parents struggled with a rocky marriage, financial problems, and his father's alcoholism. From an early age, Pollock was nurtured and influenced by his four older brothers, several of whom became interested in art. Pollock followed suit, studying sculpture and drawing as a high school student in Los Angeles. In addition to creativity, however, Pollock's family history included emotional instability. He experienced bouts of depression and drinking that began during his teen years and continued throughout his life, with only brief interludes of relative tranquility.

In 1930, a few months after he turned eighteen, Pollock joined his brothers Charles and Frank in New York City, where Charles was making inroads in the art world. In the years that followed, Pollock studied at the Art Students League under the well-known regionalist painter Thomas Hart Benton. He also benefited greatly from the art-related relief programs that were launched during the Great Depression. Pollock took free art classes, for instance, from experienced artists who received payment through state- and city-sponsored work programs. In February 1935 he got a job cleaning outdoor statues as part of a work-relief program.

Life as a WPA Artist

In the summer of 1935 Pollock became one of the 1,000 or so artists in New York to join the ranks of the newly launched Federal Art Project (FAP) of the Works Progress Administration (WPA). The FAP represented a fantastic opportunity for Pollock, who frequently stated that "I can't do anything but paint."[1] Pollock's job with the FAP enabled him to earn the relatively lavish sum of $23.86 a week (about $400 in 2012 dollars) by doing what he loved.

Pollock initially worked in the FAP mural division and assisted a more experienced artist on a project. He later transferred to the easel division, where

141

he could focus on his own works. Pollock had the good fortune to avoid the stringent "painting factory" conditions that were imposed on some easel artists in the early months of the New York project. Instead, he worked in his own studio, reported to the WPA office occasionally, and produced a minimum of about one painting per month.

The FAP energized the New York art scene during the late 1930s. Blessed with an abundance of free time and a measure of financial security, project artists gathered in the bars and cafeterias of Greenwich Village to discuss and argue about their work. This exchange of ideas created a vibrant, innovative art community. "The WPA really amounted to a graduate program in art," recalled one of the FAP artists who participated with Pollock. "It was an experience we shared. It was really the first art community I was ever aware of."[2]

Pollock remained part of the FAP for more than seven years, with only a few brief interruptions. During that period he experimented with a wide variety of techniques and ideas as he developed his own distinctive style. Without a rigorous schedule to follow, he also devoted time to museum visits and various other artistic activities. For example, he assisted in the workshop of the Mexican artist Alfaro Siqueiros in the spring of 1936. This experience helped open Pollock's eyes to the possibilities of applying paint without the use of a brush—a technique that would figure prominently in his later work.

As Pollock thrived artistically under the WPA, though, he continued to depend on others to care for him physically and emotionally. His brother Sande, a fellow FAP artist, filled that role from the mid-1930s to the early 1940s. Sande handled most of the issues of day-to-day life in the apartment they shared, and he also served as his brother's keeper by retrieving him from his frequent drinking binges. In 1941 Pollock began a relationship with his future wife, Lee Krasner, and she took over the role of his protector while trying to pursue her own art career. Despite the patient sacrifice of his brother and Krasner, however, Pollock continued to struggle with alcoholism and mental illness. He began undergoing psychiatric treatment in 1937, and he was hospitalized for more than three months in 1938 after an emotional collapse.

"The Greatest Living American Painter"

When the WPA ended in 1943, Pollock was forced to find a new means of supporting himself. His salvation came in the form of art collector and gallery owner Peggy Guggenheim, who put him on a monthly salary and began staging exhibitions of his work. In 1945 Pollock and Krasner moved to a rural farm at the eastern end of Long Island. The move gave him a new sense of stability and launched one of the most productive periods of his career.

Over the next few years Pollock's paintings moved away from representational figures and toward abstraction. In 1947 he developed the painting technique that became a hallmark of his art. He laid large pieces of unstretched canvas—some of them measuring eighteen feet in length—on the floor of his studio and used brushes and sticks to drip, pour, and fling paint onto the surface, creating evocative webs of line and color. "On the floor I am more at ease," he explained. "I feel nearer, more a part of the painting.... I can walk around it, work from the four sides and literally be *in* the painting."[3]

Pollock soon emerged as the most famous member of the abstract expressionist art movement. A 1949 article in *Life* magazine introduced him and his "action painting" technique to the general public. During this period, supportive critics and artists saddled him with titles that would prove as burdensome as they were appreciative. French artist Georges Mathieu, for instance, described Pollock as "the greatest living American painter."[4]

The critical and popular attention heaped upon Pollock aroused jealousy among fellow artists as well as opposition among traditional-minded critics. A writer for *Time,* for instance, derided the painter with the nickname "Jack the Dripper."[5] The backlash and the general pressures of celebrity proved dangerous for an individual who had always suffered from severe anxiety and self-doubt. "The more Jackson's fame grew, the more tormented he felt," Krasner later noted. "My help, support, and encouragement didn't seem to be enough."[6]

Pollock's bursts of productivity grew shorter and more infrequent during the early 1950s, while his alcohol-fueled rages became more common. By the summer of 1956, he had not painted a picture in more than a year, had separated from Krasner, and suffered from both mental and physical health issues. On the evening of August 11, after a daylong drinking binge, he was killed when he ran his car off the road near his Long Island home. The crash also took the life of one of the two young women who were passengers in the vehicle.

Pollock's violent death at age forty-four cemented his reputation as a self-destructive genius. In the decades that followed, his iconic status and Krasner's skillful management of his portfolio helped the value of Pollock paintings soar to astronomical values. His painting *Number 5, 1948* sold in 2006 for $140 million, which ranks among the highest prices ever paid for a work of art.

Sources

Engelmann, Ines Janet. *Jackson Pollock and Lee Krasner.* Munich, Germany: Prestel, 2007.
Naifeh, Steven, and Gregory White Smith. *Jackson Pollock: An American Saga.* New York: Clarkson N. Potter, 1989.
Toynton, Evelyn. *Jackson Pollock.* New Haven, CT: Yale University Press, 2012.

Notes

[1] Quoted in Naifeh, Steven, and Gregory White Smith. *Jackson Pollock: An American Saga.* New York: Clarkson N. Potter, 1989, p. 3.

[2] Quoted in Naifeh and Smith, p. 276.

[3] Quoted in Engelmann, Ines Janet. *Jackson Pollock and Lee Krasner.* Munich, Germany: Prestel, 2007, p. 47.

[4] Quoted in Friedman, B. H. *Jackson Pollock: Energy Made Visible.* New York: McGraw Hill, 1972, p. 129.

[5] Quoted in Naifeh and Smith, p. 753.

[6] Quoted in Engelmann, p. 74.

Franklin D. Roosevelt (1882-1945)
*President of the United States from 1933 to
1945 and Champion of the New Deal*

Born on January 20, 1882, Franklin Delano Roosevelt was the only son of James Roosevelt and Sara Delano Roosevelt. Both of his parents hailed from wealthy and powerful families in New York State. Roosevelt grew up on an expansive estate in Hyde Park, and he received the doting attention of his strong-willed mother throughout his youth.

After being tutored at home, Roosevelt attended the prestigious Groton School in Massachusetts and went on to graduate from Harvard University in 1904. Although he later studied at Columbia Law School, Roosevelt did not distinguish himself as a student and never received a degree from that institution. In 1905 he married Eleanor Roosevelt, his distant cousin, over the strenuous objections of his mother. Between 1906 and 1916 the couple became the parents of six children, one of whom died in infancy.

When Roosevelt (who was frequently referred to by his FDR initials) decided to enter the world of politics, he considered membership in the Republican Party. After all, former Republican president Theodore Roosevelt was his fifth cousin and Eleanor's uncle, and most of his family's wealthy friends were Republicans. Roosevelt ultimately allied himself with the Democratic Party, however, and won a seat in the New York Senate in 1910. Three years later President Woodrow Wilson appointed him assistant secretary of the U.S. Navy, and Roosevelt played a valuable administrative role during World War I. His first attempt at gaining national elective office came in 1920, when he ran as the vice presidential nominee on the Democratic ticket. Though he and running mate James M. Cox lost the election, Roosevelt's strong performance on the campaign trail enhanced his stature as a rising star in the party.

In the summer of 1921 Roosevelt experienced a devastating blow when he contracted polio and lost the use of his legs. He put his political career on hold for nearly eight years as he underwent treatment and rehabilitation. He used a wheelchair or leg braces for the rest of his life, although he largely managed to hide that fact from the public.

In addition to his fight with polio, Roosevelt went through a crisis in his personal life around this time. In the late 1910s he had entered into a romantic relationship with Lucy Mercer, who had worked as a secretary for the Roosevelt family. When Eleanor Roosevelt learned of her husband's affair, the couple came close to divorcing. Since a divorce would have dealt a severe blow to Roosevelt's political aspirations, he and his wife reached an agreement that allowed them to remain married. Eleanor helped Roosevelt adjust to his disability and revive his career in politics. In return, she freely pursued her own passions, which included outspoken support for racial equality and other social reforms. This alliance served them both well in the coming decades.

Battling the Great Depression

Roosevelt made his political comeback as a candidate in the 1928 governor's race in New York, winning the election by a narrow margin. In the years that followed, he earned a reputation as one of the nation's most effective and innovative governors in responding to the Great Depression. In 1931 he convinced the state legislature to create the Temporary Emergency Relief Administration (TERA), which offered a financial lifeline to residents who faced destitution as a result of unemployment. Before long, New York became recognized as a national leader in providing public assistance to struggling families.

Roosevelt's astute management of the state government in a time of crisis helped him claim the Democratic presidential nomination in 1932. His campaign promised voters an ambitious "New Deal" program of relief, recovery, and reform. He swept to victory in the November election, even though his New Deal was more a vague set of ideas than a concrete plan of action at that point in time.

Once he took office, however, Roosevelt proved to be a decisive, confident, and extraordinarily productive leader. During the pivotal hundred days that followed his inauguration, his administration secured the passage of fifteen major bills by Congress, which was dominated by Roosevelt's fellow Democrats at the time. One historian described this accomplishment as "the most astonishing burst of legislation in American history."[1] The New Deal profoundly changed federal regulation of financial systems, agriculture, and business, as well as federal management of public works projects and relief programs.

Although the severity of the economic crisis made it easier for Roosevelt to bring about such epic reforms, the president's keen political instincts and personal charm also contributed to his achievements. A pioneer in the use of radio communication, he used his weekly "fireside chat" broadcasts to explain his policies to the American people and to calm their fears about the difficult conditions facing the nation. "When things would get rough," one citizen remembered of Roosevelt's radio broadcasts, "he would sit down and talk to you like a daddy and tell his children 'just stick with me, things are going to get better.'"[2] Great numbers of Americans found reassurance in the simple sincerity of his words, and many came to regard Roosevelt as a friend.

Not everyone was a fan of the president, however. His expansion of the federal government's power drew criticism from both ends of the political spectrum. Critics on the right portrayed him as a dangerous radical who was intent on carrying out a socialist revolution or establishing a dictatorship. Meanwhile, critics on the far left condemned Roosevelt for trying to preserve the political, economic, and social foundations on which the country had historically rested. They claimed that his New Deal programs merely propped up a failing capitalist system that needed to be overthrown.

Roosevelt's Work-Relief Programs

Undaunted by the scale of the Depression and the diverse political forces aligned against him, Roosevelt frequently undertook what he termed "bold, persistent experimentation"[3] in launching policy initiatives and creating government agencies. Indeed, the New Deal's large-scale work-relief programs offer a prime example of Roosevelt's brand of experimentation. The president was determined to help the millions of people who were unemployed, but he rejected the more conventional approach of providing direct relief. He felt that welfare payments destroyed recipients' morale and work ethic and represented a "violation of the traditions of America."[4] Instead, he experimented by launching work-relief programs on a scale never before attempted. Under these programs, Americans would receive financial assistance in return for work that benefited the wider community.

At the same time, though, the Roosevelt administration designed the pay rates and work projects of agencies like the Works Progress Administration (WPA) so that they would not directly compete with private business. Roosevelt also cut back on WPA expenditures to reduce budget deficits.

Roosevelt's WPA did not provide work to everyone who needed it, and the inconsistent approach to funding sometimes created uncertainty and upheaval for those employed by the agency. Nonetheless, over the course of eight years the WPA provided work and hope to millions of people while also bringing new schools, bridges, roads, airports, and other infrastructure to communities nationwide.

Wartime Leader

Roosevelt faced a new crisis in the late 1930s as the threat of World War II loomed. Although isolationist sentiment ran high in the United States, he argued as early as 1937 that America and its allies had a responsibility to contain aggressive nations around the globe. Following the outbreak of hostilities in Europe in 1939, he launched a major upgrade of the nation's military capacity and began providing desperately needed armaments to the Allied countries battling Nazi Germany.

The war also helped convince Roosevelt to seek a third term in office—something no previous U.S. president had ever attempted. (The two-term limit for presidents did not take effect until 1951, when the Twenty-Second Amendment to the U.S. Constitution was ratified.) Following his reelection in 1940, he turned his attention away from the liberal reforms he had previously championed and focused on military matters. Roosevelt explained that "Dr. New Deal" had been replaced by "Dr. Win-the-War."[5]

After the Japanese attack on Pearl Harbor drew the United States into the war in December 1941, Roosevelt proved to be a shrewd commander-in-chief. His careful diplomacy helped preserve the delicate alliance between the United States, Great Britain, and the Soviet Union that led to the defeat of Nazi Germany. As the war moved into its final phase, he also helped lay the groundwork for the creation of the United Nations. A few of Roosevelt's war-related actions were less admirable, however, including his decision to confine Japanese Americans in internment camps and his failure to act more decisively to aid victims of the Holocaust.

Still, Roosevelt's wartime leadership earned the respect and admiration of many American citizens. He won reelection to a fourth term in office in 1944, even though he was in visibly poor health by that point. He served only three months of his final term before he died of a cerebral hemorrhage on April 12, 1945, while vacationing in Warm Springs, Georgia.

Sources

Brands, H. W. *Traitor to His Class: The Privileged Life and Radical Presidency of Franklin Delano Roosevelt*. New York: Doubleday, 2008.

Hamby, Alonzo L. *For the Survival of Democracy: Franklin Roosevelt and the World Crisis of the 1930s.* New York: Free Press, 2004.

Leuchtenburg, William E. *The FDR Years: On Roosevelt and His Legacy.* New York: Columbia University Press, 1995.

Renshaw, Patrick. *Franklin D. Roosevelt.* Harlow, UK: Longman, 2004.

Notes

[1] Renshaw, Patrick. *Franklin D. Roosevelt.* Harlow, UK: Longman, 2004, p. 87.

[2] Bindas, Kenneth. *Remembering the Great Depression in the Rural South.* Gainesville: University Press of Florida, 2007, p. 40.

[3] Quoted in DiNunzio, Mario R. *Franklin D. Roosevelt and the Third American Revolution.* Santa Barbara, CA: Praeger, 2011, p. 48.

[4] Roosevelt, Franklin D. *The Public Papers and Addresses of Franklin D. Roosevelt,* Vol. 4. New York: Random House, 1938, pp. 19-20.

[5] Roosevelt, Franklin D. Excerpts from the Press Conference, December 28, 1943. The American Presidency Project. Retrieved from http://www.presidency.ucsb.edu.

Orson Welles (1915-1985)
Director and Actor in the WPA Federal Theatre Project

George Orson Welles was born on May 6, 1915, in Kenosha, Wisconsin. His parents separated when he was six years old and both died a few years later. This upheaval in his life, however, did nothing to inhibit the startling intelligence that he demonstrated from his earliest years. "Everybody told me from the moment I could hear that I was absolutely marvelous,"[1] Welles later noted.

Welles ended up focusing his talents on the arts. He scored his first major success at age sixteen when, during a trip to Ireland, he landed an important role in a Shakespearen production at the Gate Theatre in Dublin. Upon returning to the United States in 1932, Welles hoped to find similar success on the stages of New York. By that time, though, the Great Depression had caused widespread unemployment and financial ruin. With the theater world feeling the effects of the severe economic downturn, it took Welles two years to land a part in a New York play.

Joins the Federal Theater Project

Welles's job prospects took a decided turn for the better in 1935, when the efforts of the Works Progress Administration (WPA) helped revive American theater. Many of the people who went to work for the Federal Theatre Project (FTP) of the WPA in New York were destitute by the time they received work relief. Welles, on the other hand, had found work as a radio actor, and his deep, resonant voice was in such demand that he was earning the lavish salary of around $1,000 per week.

In order to join the FTP, Welles had to be hired under a rule that allowed up to 10 percent of a project's employees to come from outside the relief rolls. Such positions were hard to come by, and Welles landed one only because of his friendship with theater producer and director John Houseman. Even though Welles had little directing experience, Houseman handed his protégé the job of directing a play for the FTP Negro Theatre Unit in Harlem. Welles was only twenty years old when rehearsals got underway in early 1936.

The "Wonder Boy" at Work

Over the next year and a half, the young director demonstrated such prodigious talent that he earned the nickname "Wonder Boy Welles."[2] His first production was Shakespeare's *Macbeth,* but Welles transformed the play by setting it in Haiti. The setting enabled him to create a sultry production, complete with a jungle castle, elements of voodoo, and a troupe of African drummers.

Although there was a certain amount of tension as the young, white, wealthy director supervised an African-American cast at a theater in the heart of Harlem, Welles proved equal to the task. He managed to create a sense of community among the company, partly by turning the late-night rehearsals into a party and paying for the food and drinks out of his own pocket. The end result was a smash hit that helped prove the legitimacy of the FTP. *Macbeth* sold out its entire original run of sixty-four shows and was later performed on the road by a touring company.

With this success under their belts, Welles and Houseman gained the freedom to form a new FTP unit, Project 891. They immediately veered off in new directions, staging the madcap farce *Horse Eats Hat* followed by the Elizabethan play *Doctor Faustus.* Although Welles took a role in the cast of both productions, his directorial abilities garnered the most attention. As he had done with *Macbeth,* he radically reconfigured the original plays, introduced innovative sets and lighting, and nurtured, cajoled, and intimidated his actors into fulfilling his vision for the works. Welles's accomplishments were all the more impressive given his hectic schedule. Between his radio work and his FTP responsibilities, he often worked around the clock. "In those days," he later recalled, "I seemed to be able to go without any sleep at all."[3]

Welles's resourcefulness enabled him to use the FTP system to great dramatic advantage. Like most WPA projects, the FTP productions employed an abundance of people. Welles took the opportunity to stage highly involved shows featuring numerous roles and technical effects. *Horse Eats Hat,* for instance, featured seventy-four actors and an army of technicians. Welles also took advantage of the same WPA rule that he had used to gain entrance to the FTP to fill leading roles in his productions with experienced actors. "The backbone of the WPA," he later observed, "was actors who really had money from other sources."[4]

The King of Controversy

Welles's FTP experience also taught him how controversy could be valuable as a public relations tool. *The Cradle Will Rock*—a leftist musical written by Marc Blitzstein, a musician and composer who dreamed of a coming Marxist revolution—gave Welles's career a major boost. Welles took up the play in the spring of 1937, inspired by the challenge of turning it into a glitzy Broadway extravaganza. When the WPA attempted to shut down the play because of its controversial pro-union content, Welles and Houseman defied the ban and arranged an impromptu performance. Though it did not include the show-stopping production elements that Welles had designed, the performance nonetheless created a great sensation and generated a great deal of publicity.

Welles resigned from the FTP a short time later, but the fame he had gained during his time with the theater project provided him with numerous other opportunities. He and Houseman teamed up again to launch the Mercury Theatre, a commercial operation that encompassed both stage productions and radio plays. Its famous 1938 radio broadcast of *The War of the Worlds* brought Welles one of his greatest moments of notoriety. When Mercury actors presented a series of mock news reports about an alien invasion in progress, it created mass hysteria as thousands of listeners mistakenly believed that the reports were real. The first Mercury stage plays enjoyed success as well, but Welles's habit of staging elaborate productions proved financially dangerous for a private enterprise. When two successive plays flopped in 1938 and 1939, the Mercury Theatre was forced to close its doors.

In 1940 Welles headed for Hollywood to try his hand at moviemaking. His first film was *Citizen Kane,* a fictional story based on the life of newspaper publisher William Randolph Hearst. Welles co-wrote, directed, and starred in the film, which has been cited by many critics as one of the greatest movies ever made. *Citizen Kane* was a box-office disappointment at the time of its release, however, partly because the wealthy and powerful Hearst opposed it every step of the way.

Although Welles's first film is widely considered a masterpiece, the controversy surrounding it marked the beginning of his decline. Movie studios became leery of granting him a free hand, and he often struggled to retain creative control of his films. Welles ended up working largely outside of the Hollywood studio system in the years that followed, which made it more difficult to obtain funding for his projects. He still managed to produce several highly acclaimed works, including *The Magnificent Ambersons* (1942) and *Touch of Evil* (1958).

Despite the difficulties he faced as a filmmaker, Welles remained a celebrity for the rest of his life. A popular film actor, he also undertook occasional directing and acting jobs in the theater. He gained further attention from his brief marriage to movie star Rita Hayworth in the mid-1940s and later from his appearances on television talk shows and in wine commercials. His fame did not diminish the sense of disappointment that surrounded his later life, however. After suffering from obesity and poor health for a number of years, Welles died on October 10, 1985, at the age of seventy.

Sources

Callow, Simon. *Orson Welles: The Road to Xanadu.* London: Cape, 1995.

Leaming, Barbara. *Orson Welles: A Biography.* New York: Limelight, 1995.

Notes

[1] Quoted in "The Battle over *Citizen Kane*." Public Broadcasting Service, n.d. Retrieved from http://www.pbs.org/wgbh/amex/kane2.

[2] Quoted in Leaming, Barbara. *Orson Welles: A Biography.* New York: Limelight, 1995, p. 113.

[3] Quoted in Leaming, p. 103.

[4] Quoted in Leaming, p. 113.

Ellen S. Woodward (1887-1971)
Director of the Women's Division of the Works Progress Administration

Ellen Woodward was born as Ellen Sullivan on July 11, 1887, in Oxford, Mississippi. Both of her parents hailed from wealthy, prominent, and politically active Southern families. "I grew up in an atmosphere of politics," she recalled, "where governmental affairs—local, state, and national—were constantly discussed."[1] Those discussions were largely directed by her father, William Van Amberg Sullivan, a lawyer who was active in the Democratic Party and served in the U.S. Congress from 1897 to 1900.

In 1906 Ellen married Albert Woodward. They settled in Louisville, Mississippi, and had a son. Her husband, a lawyer with political aspirations, won a seat in the state legislature in 1923. After serving less than two years in office, however, he died from a heart attack. Woodward, who had remained active in civic affairs as a member of women's clubs, was elected to complete her husband's term. She thus became the third woman ever to serve in the Mississippi House of Representatives. After her term ended, Woodward went on to work for the Mississippi State Board of Development.

By the early 1930s Woodward had emerged as an influential voice among the state's Democrats. She used her influence to support Franklin D. Roosevelt in the 1932 presidential election, and her efforts put her in good graces with the new administration. Harry Hopkins, director of the Federal Emergency Relief Administration (FERA), summoned Woodward to Washington in August 1933 to take charge of the Women's Division of the FERA.

Director of Women's Relief

Charming, polite, and always impeccably dressed, Woodward struck many of her New Deal colleagues as the embodiment of Southern grace. Yet she was also a hard-charging administrator whom one colleague described as "a demon for work."[2] Woodward led the efforts of several federal agencies, including the FERA and the Civil Works Administration (CWA), to provide work relief to American women. She was ultimately named the head of the Women's Division of the Works Progress Administration (WPA) in 1935. (The department was later renamed the Division of Women's and Professional Projects.)

Regardless of which agency she worked for, Woodward grappled with a basic problem: many of the officials involved in public relief—particularly those at the state and local levels—believed that providing jobs to women was less important than providing jobs to men. That attitude stemmed from the traditional belief that men served as family breadwinners. It often resulted in policies and decisions that made it more difficult for women to receive work relief and limited the types of jobs they could perform.

Despite such difficulties, Woodward plowed ahead and made notable progress. Within five months of her arrival in Washington, 300,000 women had received jobs through the FERA and the CWA. The effort expanded after the launch of the WPA in 1935. At its peak level of female employment in early 1936, the agency was providing work to 440,000 women. To achieve her mission, Woodward drew on the support of key allies like first lady Eleanor Roosevelt, who used her influence to advance projects that used women workers and clear obstacles related to female employment.

Because construction and many other work categories were deemed off-limits to women, Woodward and her staff focused on creating jobs in fields that had traditionally accepted women, such as nursing, library work, teaching, and food preparation. The WPA program that provided lunches to schoolchildren became one of the most popular initiatives of the Women's Division. In fact, it served as the forerunner to school nutrition projects that have continued to the present day. In another innovative effort, the WPA established cooperatives to process surplus farm products that had been purchased by the government's Agricultural Adjustment Administration. This effort put women to work canning food and making mattresses, and the finished products were distributed to relief recipients.

Woodward employed a similar approach in establishing thousands of WPA sewing centers to produce sheets, blankets, and other items for struggling families. Sewing provided a practical solution to a difficult problem: nearly four out of five women on relief were unskilled, and many of them had never worked outside the home. A large percentage had experience in sewing, however, or could quickly learn the skill. As a result, sewing occupied more than half of the agency's female work force, and such positions helped increase recipients' self-confidence as well as their income. "I don't think you have any idea what they have done to women," one observer said of the sewing centers. "They come in sullen, dejected, half starved. Working in pleasant surroundings, having some money and food have done wonders to restore their health and morale."[3] Woodward also oversaw an initiative that trained women to work as domestic servants. The effort was largely unsuccessful, though, because few women were interested in entering a low-status occupation in which the number of available jobs was rapidly declining.

The WPA Arts Projects and Political Controversy

As a WPA division director who was frequently in the news, Woodward became one of the most prominent women involved in the New Deal. Her stature increased further in 1936, when she took on the added responsibility of overseeing the four Federal One arts programs of the WPA: the Federal Writers' Project, Federal Theatre Project, Federal Music Project, and Federal Art Project. Woodward found the new position to be a political minefield. In 1937 she had to deal with militant protests staged by members of the arts programs. The following year she was drawn into the congressional investigation of alleged communist subversion in the Federal Theatre and Writers' Projects.

In December 1938 Woodward testified before the House Un-American Activities Committee (HUAC). She not only defended the WPA arts programs and refuted allegations of radical activity but she also sharply criticized the committee and its tactics. The legislators simply brushed aside her testimony, however, and HUAC regularly claimed that the WPA arts programs were riddled with communists.

Woodward's appearance before HUAC came near the end of her tenure with the WPA. A few weeks later, she left the agency when President Roosevelt appointed her as a member of the Social Security Board. Although the reasons for the reassignment were never stated, some historians believe that she was eased out of the WPA as part of a larger shakeup caused by the departure of Harry Hopkins and the growing conservative opposition to the New Deal.

During her eight years on the Social Security Board, Woodward worked to provide a larger share of social insurance benefits to women. She also collaborated with other female members of the Roosevelt administration in an effort to maintain and expand the number of women in government service. Woodward closed out her career in the Office of International Relations of the

Federal Security Agency, where she coordinated relief efforts outside the United States. Following her retirement in 1953, she continued to live in Washington. She remained active in Democratic politics until her health began failing in the early 1960s. Woodward passed away on September 23, 1971, at the age of eighty-four.

Sources

Swain, Martha H. *Ellen S. Woodward: New Deal Advocate for Women.* Jackson: University Press of Mississippi, 1995.

Ware, Susan. *Beyond Suffrage: Women in the New Deal.* Cambridge, MA: Harvard University Press, 1981.

Notes

[1] Quoted in Swain, Martha H. *Ellen S. Woodward: New Deal Advocate for Women.* Jackson: University Press of Mississippi, 1995, p. 4.

[2] Quoted in Swain, p. 61.

[3] Quoted in Swain, p. 53.

PRIMARY SOURCES

Chronicling the Difficulties of Depression-Era Unemployment

In 1931 journalist Adela Rogers St. Johns spent several weeks investigating Depression-era unemployment and relief conditions in Los Angeles by posing as a jobless resident who had been reduced to destitution. In the following excerpt from her multi-part exposé published in the Los Angeles Examiner, *she describes the lack of employment opportunities, the physical hardships endured by female job-seekers, and small but meaningful acts of kindness from strangers.*

The excerpt concludes with an account of her experience with the Community Chest, the local charity responsible for managing relief efforts in the city. Because she had adopted the persona of a woman recently arrived in the city, St. Johns is labeled a "transient"—someone who travels from city to city in search of work. During the Depression, the Community Chest and other local aid agencies often refused to provide relief assistance to transients.

I didn't have a nickel. By the spirit of my compact to go as thousands of women today are going to seek work, I didn't have a friend among the million and a quarter people in the city of Los Angeles. I was starting from scratch, no money, no baggage, no friends.

I had to get work if I wanted to eat, to sleep, to keep warm.

Not work next week, nor next month, nor when things "get better." Cold and hunger will not wait. Yet I was to discover later that both cold and hunger can be borne with a grin. There are things which happen to an unemployed woman which are so much worse that cold and hunger pale into insignificance.

Burning Feet

Your spirit bears the humiliation of asking charity. You grow used to the yearning for brightness and gaiety. You warm your icy loneliness, your homelessness, at the beacon fires of kindness and sympathy which spring up all along the way.

But nothing, nothing, seems to take away the agony of aching, sore, burning feet.

Grotesque, isn't it?

Feet that scream in protest every time they touch another foot of the miles and miles of pavement that lie between one employment agency and another, one breadline and another, one possible job and another, one charity organization and another.

There are ten thousand—twenty thousand—nobody knows just how many thousands of unemployed girls and women in this city. With a brave grin—many of them are brave and kind—or with a bitter sneer, for they grow bitter as they tramp the pavements and listen to the purr of automobile tires and the clang of street car bells, they will say to you, "I'll be all right if my feet hold out."

You see them slipping off worn, down-at-the-heel shoes, rubbing the sore and aching places with a tenderness that is terrible and pitiful. Some of them look at you with real pain in their eyes and say, "Gee, I can't go no further. My feet's killin' me." It isn't pretty. It isn't picturesque. But it is the whole horror of unemployment concentrated in one true, ugly picture.

My feet grew to be a throbbing menace that swamped my courage, my efficiency, my attempt to be gay....

I wanted work.

Just a chance to earn my living. Of course, I didn't intend to be fussy. I'd take any kind of a job. But I was pretty cocky about it in my secret heart. I would get work. Why not? I was young, strong, fairly intelligent and not repulsive....

I could cook. Not expertly, but well enough for the average American family.

I could wash and iron (and did I wash and iron before I was through!), sweep and make beds, darn stockings, all those things, thanks to a wise, old-fashioned grandmother.

I was expert with kids, big and little.

I was a fair typist, could type well and fast and take dictation slowly. I couldn't add but perhaps that wouldn't matter. It didn't. I was able to add everything I got hold of without trouble.

It seemed to me that was the average equipment of the average unemployed woman.

Later, a stately, gray-haired, harassed woman at the Community Chest told me with a sigh, "My good woman, there are ten thousand cooks out of work in Los Angeles."

Must Be Experts

And the head of a large commercial employment agency shook her head and said harshly:

"No good sending you out unless you're very expert. Only the best get jobs now—and most of them don't."

She didn't send me out....

In the first agency I tried I became familiar with the "board." Upon a blackboard in every agency are written down the jobs open. I looked eagerly, my hopes leaping as I saw any number of them—maids, cooks, mother's helpers.

A tall blond giggled as she saw my face light up.

"Don't pay any attention to those," she said. "That one's been there since before Hoover passed the first war debt. They just keep 'em there to make things look good."

In that first agency I got a wallop right on the chin.

From behind the desk a tall old woman looked me over.

"Where's your references?" she said. "Got any?"

"No."

"Don't waste my time," she said. "I've got two thousand girls registered here that've got references from Mrs. Vanderbilt and Mary Pickford."

Down the long, narrow, dark stairs. Up another pair exactly like them. On the board, "Waitresses." It seemed simple.

The man stared at me.

"Can't you read," he said. "Don't it say 18 and very snappy? If you can't read, don't come around."

As I turned away, a little sick, a pretty little Spanish girl spoke to me.

"Say, them waitress jobs are fierce. Last one I tried for, they made me strip to my pants and brassiere to see if I could stand the uniform. I didn't get the job neither."

A Kindly Woman

But the next woman was kind. Very kind. A big woman with rings on her hands, a dark green smock buttoned over her portly figure, a cigaret in her mouth, and kind eyes.

"Something happened to you, hasn't it?" she said.

"Yes," I told her.

She flipped through a file.

"Here's a job at housework. Go out there. Never mind the commission. If you get the job, I'll take it out of your first week's salary. It's a bum place, but you might get a little stake. She'll want you to clean apartments. Can you do that?" ...

"I'll go," I said.

"Got car fare?"

I shook my head.

Gives Her Quarter

From a worn and overstuffed purse she took a quarter.

"Here you are," she said. "Good luck, sister."

I spent a nickel of that for coffee. I went on a long journey and walked seven blocks to a small, strange, pink stucco house. A blonde woman with untidy hair came to the door. I showed her my card. My feet hurt a little. She looked at the card, not at me.

"That position's been filled for a week," she said, and shut the door in my face.

Slowly, I walked back to the car line. I had a dime left. I was hungry. The hours stretched ahead, long and cold and friendless.

I decided to walk back to town to save the dime. One slim, rather dirty dime. It stood between me—and I didn't know what.

I walked swiftly, then more slowly. My feet began to hurt. Long, long blocks. I asked two women for a ride, but they didn't stop. I got back to town....

At 6 o'clock, the city changes. Doors close. The crowds seem to grow less friendly. I was dirty, tired, hungry. And I knew of not one door that was open to me....

I had clung to my dime. My last dime. You use that phrase often, lightly, easily. I'll never use it again. Not me. That dime felt good between my fingers— it felt warm. I kept it until after midnight.

At 6 o'clock I knew I was hungry. My insides ached. My head felt funny. But I was afraid to spend any money. The library was open and I went in there and read. It was warm. I counted over a hundred women, who looked hungry, too. Restless and hungry. They kept their eyes on their books or their papers. One or two of them dozed.

Suddenly it occurred to me to call the Community Chest.…

The Community Chest did not answer.

Under the heading "Y. W. C. A." I found the address of a hotel on Figueroa street. That might be a relief station. Again I walked. The blocks are so long. You try to pretend each time that you only have to go one block. It seems shorter that way. I walked into the lobby. Bright, beautiful, with bellboys in natty uniforms, ladies in evening dress, Christmas trees. My shabbiness stood out against it like a ragged banner. Three times I walked across that lobby, trying to get up the courage to speak to the clerk. Conscious of my old shoes, my old hat, my worn gloves, my empty pocketbook.

That is the first step down, that feeling of shabbiness. It burns like a brand. You think people are staring at you, making fun of you, wondering how you have the nerve to be there.

In an employment agency I sat staring at the floor. The woman next to me shifted, gave me a hot look. Then, suddenly, with tears streaming down her face, she said, "Look at my stockings! Go ahead and look. Look at them. I've darned them and darned them—"

I hadn't even seen her stockings. But she wore them with their holes and mended runs, as Hester wore the scarlet letter. The badge of her shame. The shame of poverty, of unemployment. There should be no shame to poverty. But there is.

Gets You Down
Shame of Poverty Rubbed in by Charity Workers

It gets you down. The people who work to help the unemployed should remember that, always. To lose courage is to lose the battle. To feel charity rubbed into the sore wounds of your loneliness and panic is the worst thing that can happen.

At 848 Flower street, there is a soup kitchen for women. The lunches are wonderful. You get a ticket from the Government employment bureau, you go there, and your body is fed. But more than that, your spirit is fed. You are treated as an equal. The day I was there, a photographer came in to take pictures. Mrs. Gifford, who runs it, came in and spoke to the girls.

"You are my guests here," she said. "If you hesitate to have pictures taken, I will not allow it to be done. But there is nothing to be ashamed of, in being caught in this great depression. And perhaps when others see what we are doing here, we will get donations. But you are my guests—and you shall say."

Heads went up. A woman next to me said, gasping, "Isn't that wonderful?" It was. More wonderful than the food.

I went out into the night from that hotel trembling. It wasn't their fault. I shall tell you later of the work the Y. W. C. A. is doing. But somehow, somewhere, there should be an emergency station for women....

Until 2 o'clock I walked the streets. I was afraid to speak to a policeman. What happened to "vagrants?" Was I a vagrant? What would they do to me for begging alone in the streets at that hour?

At 2 o'clock I saw lights across my dark path. I wanted a drink of water. The wide doors of a big white garage yawned. Perhaps there somebody would give me water. I put on a bold front. I would pretend I was just on my way home from late work.

A slim, dark young man in a white linen suit met me as I came in. I opened my mouth to tell my story—to keep up my pride.

"What's wrong lady?" he said.

The lady did it. I broke!

"Could you tell me—any place where—I could get a bed to sleep, for nothing? I—I've been to the mission and I've been to the cheap hotels. I'm afraid of them."

He didn't bat an eyelash. No false sympathy.

"There's a limousine over in that corner. Got some good cushions. If you're out of it by 7 o'clock, you can sleep there."

I sought the back of that limousine as though it had been a bed of roses.

"Good night," Said the tall young man. "Have a good sleep."

That was his last word. When I went out in the morning, rumpled, dirty, disheveled, but rested, he just nodded....

I started again the weary round of employment agencies. I was still on my own, still not asking for charity. You have no idea how you cling to that.

Feels Unkempt
Sneaks Into Big Hotel and Cleans Up in Washroom

I felt dirty and unkempt. I longed for a jar of cold cream almost as much as I longed for breakfast. A glance into a store window mirror showed me a lined, dirty face, rumpled clothes, straggling hair. Not much of a front. I didn't know where to go to clean up. The splendid doorway of a big hotel stood open. Like a criminal, I glanced around. Then I sneaked in. The doorman stared at me. I tried to give him glance for glance, to look as though I had business there. After a moment, he winked. An old man, in a tall hat.

In the warm, white, sweet-smelling dressing room I made a sort of toilette.

Across the street was a coffee shop. I will never forget the man who ran that place. At the counter I ordered coffee and toast. I felt sure the girl would ask for money first, but she didn't. A large man next to me had a side order of fried potatoes, with his ham and eggs. He left them. Carefully, when no one was looking, I sneaked them and ate them with relish. A big "15" was scrawled on my check.

With hands that trembled and heart beating hard, I walked to the desk. It was a strange thing, but you get that way. The first time I asked for money in the street, I thought I was going to faint.

I laid the check on the counter and waited. The man looked at me.

"I haven't any money," I said.

Never have I seen such a look of disgust on any human countenance. With utter weariness he picked up the check and stuck it on the hook, said not a word.

"I'm sorry," I said miserably. "I'll pay you back when I get a job."

"That's only the two hundred and tenth of those I've got," he said. "Well— did you get enough to eat? I suppose you might as well owe me a quarter. Tell the girl to give you an egg and another cup of coffee."

All the time he looked as though he could cheerfully drown me. But I ate the egg....

I did not find a single commercial agency in Los Angeles which would even register me.

You cannot blame them.

One woman said to me, "We have over two thousand girls registered here whom we know well. We have placed them before. Fifteen hundred of them need work badly. We must take care of them first...."

I answered ads all day. I walked miles. The last commercial agency I tried was a small one. I told the woman there I would do anything and she sent me out on a job—which was already filled.

No Ego Left
All Look Same When Tired, Dirty, Hungry

I do not think I ever had much ego. If I had any, it is now a cold corpse. Not one of the people in employment agencies, in charity organizations, ever noticed me. Not one of them discovered in me any signs of anything different. Just remember that, you women who are today warm and comfortable. Take away your good clothes, your name, your position, and see the face the world presents....

Broke, shabby, down and out, gray with fatigue, disheveled by my days in the army of the unemployed women, I appealed at last to charity....

I cannot describe to you the feeling of humiliation, of actual guilt that welled up inside me as I walked through the gate of charity into that land where a woman abandons her pride, her inalienable rights and much of life's sweetness. And where of all places, she should be treated with the kindliness her bruised spirit demands....

Because I knew that the Community Chest headed all disbursements of funds collected to help the poor and suffering, I looked up their address in the telephone book....

I took the street car and went to the Bradbury Building—that stately and magnificent old edifice that reminded me sadly as I walked through it of days when the City of the Angels moved at a slower and more gentle pace. Reminded me of old and golden days of California, when every door was open to the stranger and hospitality was simple and sweet.

Upstairs I found a big, bright office, packed with people. Men and women. Children. Babies. Mexicans and negroes. Cripples and old folks. Men who looked like bums and women with thin faces and nervous, frightened eyes.

On all sides were glass windows and in each small office sat a woman, endlessly interviewing those who had come to ask for aid.

I arrived a few minutes before 10....

Finally, at 4 o'clock, I was ushered into an office. A tall, gray-haired woman in black motioned me to a chair. She looked so tired, so harassed, so worn, that I felt much sorrier for her than she seemed to feel for me.

She didn't look at me. I am not sure that for the first five minutes she knew whether I was black or white. Not that it mattered. Either way, I was a suffering human being.

"Transient"
Denizen of Some Strange Half-World

I explained my case. I had been here three months. I had not been able to find work. My landlady had been obliged to put me out. Without realizing it, I found I was pulling at the fingers of my shabby gloves, as I had seen so many other women do....

She wrote things on a card.

Then she said:

"We cannot do anything for you. We have no provision for transients."

That word—transient. Once you get yourself under that heading, you fall into a strange half-world, a limbo of apparently forgotten souls.

"Unless you have been a resident here for three years, you are not within our province. We simply turn you over to the County Charities."

I winced. For days, as I rubbed shoulders with all kinds of men and women in the milling mobs of the unemployed, I had heard of the County Charities. They speak of it with bated breath and a sort of horror. Perhaps they are wrong, but among the women I met the feeling was universal.

I had reached the County Charities, myself.

"Go there in the morning," the woman said, handing me a slip. "They will arrange to deport you back to your home." ...

Deport. Deport? The word hurt. I resented it with sudden bitterness. You see, your nerves get as tired as your body. You are susceptible to every little thing. Women aren't made to stand the racket of existence like men.

"But," I said, "surely you have some means to care for me here. I am a stranger; I do not know what to do—"

"We don't want strangers here," she said impatiently. "We have to take care of our own people. We are not able to care for transients. You shouldn't have come in the first place."

Sources

St. Johns, Adela Rogers. *Los Angeles Examiner.* "How Jobless, Hungry Girls Live," December 20, 1931, pp. 1, 6. "'Penniless Woman' Fed by Stranger, Sleeps in Auto," December 21, 1931, sec. 2, p. 12. "Any Woman Can Eat, Sleep if She Knows How to Do Housework, Writer Finds," December 22, 1931, sec. 2, pp. 1, 14. "Writer Forced to Charity; Meets Bar as Transient," December 24, 1931, sec. 2, pp. 1, 14.

Walter Lippmann Urges a New Approach to Work Relief

In the following December 1934 installment of his influential newspaper column "Today and Tomorrow," political commentator Walter Lippmann addresses the subject of work relief. Pointing out flaws in the design of the Public Works Administration (PWA) and the Civil Works Administration (CWA), he argues that the best approach for ending unemployment and invigorating the economy is to create a jobs program that pays reduced wages and undertakes a broad range of projects that contribute to the public good. This column was written shortly before the creation of the Works Progress Administration (WPA), but it anticipates many elements of that agency's operations, particularly its relatively low "security wage" pay structure and its emphasis on inexpensive infrastructure projects.

It is generally assumed that the alternative to a dole, that is, direct relief measured by the minimum needs of the unemployed, is either a public works program in the manner of PWA or a lot of useless activities intended to look like real work though they deceive nobody. The phrase, "public works," calls up in most minds either some elaborate project which will take years to finish and will cost millions of the taxpayers' money to operate, or else a picture of men raking dead leaves in a city park from one side of the path to the other.

The PWA as an instrument of recovery must be put down as worse than a failure. It can be shown, I think, that Mr. [Harold L.] Ickes has created an organization and a procedure which is a vast improvement on the old pork barrel and has thus made a useful reform in the normal procedure of the Federal government. But as an emergency device for creating work and priming the pump, PWA has a sorry record. The amount of net additional employment created is negligible. What is much worse, the PWA, by a wholly misconceived policy as to wages, and handicapped by the mistakes of the NRA in fixing prices, has tended to peg construction costs at a level where private reemployment is not profitable. This is illustrated by an example cited in Professor Sumner Slichter's recent book called "Towards Stability," where in the South workers on PWA projects were paid $1.00 an hour while union men on private construction were striking for 75 cents an hour.

* * *

A much more successful attempt to create work promptly was made by the CWA last winter and the general public has never properly appreciated the variety and the amount of useful work done by the CWA. Any one who wishes to get an impression of that should look at the photographic history of CWA in a volume called "America Fights the Depression."

But CWA had one deep and destructive effect. It obtained its funds from PWA and had, therefore, to adopt the wage rates set by PWA. The result was that CWA workers earned higher rate of pay per hour, but, because they were getting relief, were not allowed to earn it many hours a week. From the point of view of the work done this meant that the cost was high; from the point of view of the workers it meant that they could get a bare living by working only a few days a week. So the projects were expensive, and those who were content with a bare subsistence could obtain it by working a few days and idling the rest of the week. The system destroyed incentive to work and yet made the work costly. This, plus the inevitable errors of hasty improvisation and inadequate supervision and direction, was the ground of the justifiable complaints which were brought against CWA in all parts of the country.

* * *

If we examine the errors of PWA and CWA, it becomes clear, I think, that they arose from a failure to recognize that in a depression men cannot sell their goods or their services at pre-depression prices. If they insist on pre-depression prices for goods, they do not sell them. If they insist on pre-depression wages, they become unemployed. Both PWA and CWA were ruined by the fallacy current in all depressions, that a little work or a small volume of sales at a high rate is preferable to much work or a large volume of sales at a lower rate. It is a fallacy not confined to PWA or CWA or the trade unions. It prevailed among most business men when the codes were written.

* * *

In the past, when trade was depressed and men could not find work, they migrated to new lands. The United States was settled by a migration of this sort. Now when men moved out into new lands, they worked for what they could get. The West would not have been opened if the pioneers had insisted immediately upon work at the same rate of pay per hour as prevailed in the older settled communities from which they came.

A government public works program to deal with unemployment should be looked upon as a modern equivalent for the opening up of new lands to settlement. The government creates industrial opportunity by using cheap money to promote projects which, like the cultivation of new lands, add to the national wealth. Looked at this way, the rate of pay on emergency public works ought to be decisively lower than in established industries, but there ought to be enough of it so that a man working steadily will earn a weekly income larger than he could get from a dole or from partial employment.

A public works program based on this principle would have low labor costs. Valuable projects could be made economically sound on this level of costs. It would, therefore, not be really expensive. It would at the same time be based on the only sane theory of reward which is that the more a man works the more he earns. It would do away with the lunatic theory that the way to increase jobs is to limit work. It would supply the only fair and searching test of whether a man actually wanted work or preferred to be supported by charity. It would put to the union leaders the practical question as to whether they prefer high rates and little work and therefore meager annual incomes.

Such a public works program would be a radically different thing from that of PWA. It could attack urban and rural slums with a fair prospect of being able to make the new houses self-supporting. This is something that private capital can scarcely hope to do. It could build sewers and sewage plants, waterworks and other municipal projects at a cost which cities could bear. It could carry electricity into the country districts at a cost far below that which now prevails. Such a program would have, of course, to be accompanied by a reduction in the monopolistic prices of materials.

The great virtue of such a program is that it could become a powerful influence in bringing the national economy into balance at the point where it is now most unbalanced. If that can be done, the balancing of the budget will present no difficulties. On the other hand, if the economy is not balanced, it is a safe prediction that the budget will not long stay balanced.

Those who take this view will not test the forthcoming budget by looking to see whether the deficit is to be two billions for direct relief or four billions for public works and relief. They will look to see whether the economic policy of the public works program, specifically as to wages and prices of materials, is one designed to stabilize the present maladjustments or to correct them. For in the long run two billions spent unwisely would be far more expensive than four billions spent with the deliberate purpose of removing the cause of unemployment.

Source

Lippmann, Walter. "Today and Tomorrow." *Hartford Courant,* December 27, 1934, p. 12.

President Roosevelt Discusses the Works Progress Administration

Throughout his presidency, Franklin D. Roosevelt used his "Fireside Chat" radio broadcasts to explain his policies to the nation. In the broadcast he delivered on April 28, 1935, he devoted particular attention to his administration's greatly expanded work relief initiatives, which would soon be led by the Works Progress Administration (WPA). The president's fireside chat laid out many of the principles that would guide the work of the WPA, and it also reflects the degree to which plans for the program were still in a state of flux. For instance, the full Works Progress Administration name had not yet been established. Instead, the agency is referred to the "Progress Division." Also, Roosevelt's description of its responsibilities is somewhat more limited than the expansive operation that would be established in the following months.

My most immediate concern is in carrying out the purposes of the great work program just enacted by the Congress. Its first objective is to put men and women now on the relief rolls to work and, incidentally, to assist materially in our already unmistakable march toward recovery. I shall not confuse my discussion by a multitude of figures. So many figures are quoted to prove so many things. Sometimes it depends upon what paper you read and what broadcast you hear.

Therefore, let us keep our minds on two or three simple essential facts in connection with this problem of unemployment. It is true that while business and industry are definitely better our relief rolls are still too large. However, for the first time in five years the relief rolls have declined instead of increased during the winter months. They are still declining. The simple fact is that many millions more people have private work today than two years ago today or one year ago today and every day that passes offers more chances to work for those who want to work. In spite of the fact that unemployment remains a serious problem here as in every other Nation, we have come to recognize the possibility and the necessity of certain helpful remedial measures.

These measures are of two kinds. The first is to make provisions intended to relieve, to minimize, and to prevent future unemployment; the second is to establish the practical means to help those who are unemployed in this present emergency. Our social security legislation is an attempt to answer the first of these questions; our Works Relief program, the second.

The program for social security now pending before the Congress is a necessary part of the future unemployment policy of the Government. While our present and projected expenditures for work relief are wholly within the reasonable limits of our national credit resources, it is obvious that we cannot continue to create governmental deficits for that purpose year after year. We must begin now to make provision for the future. That is why our social security program is an important part of the complete picture. It proposes, by means of old-age pensions, to help those who have reached the age of retirement to give up their jobs and thus give to the younger generation greater opportunities for work and to give to all a feeling of security as they look toward old age.

The unemployment insurance part of the legislation will not only help to guard the individual in future periods of lay-off against dependence upon relief, but it will, by sustaining purchasing power, cushion the shock of economic distress. Another helpful feature of unemployment insurance is the incentive it will give to employers to plan more carefully in order that unemployment may be prevented by the stabilizing of employment itself.

Provisions for social security, however, are protections for the future. Our responsibility for the immediate necessities of the unemployed has been met by the Congress through the most comprehensive work plan in the history of the Nation. Our problem is to put to work three and one-half million employable persons now on the relief rolls. It is a problem quite as much for private industry as for the Government.

We are losing no time getting the Government's vast work relief program under way and we have every reason to believe that it should be in full swing by autumn. In directing it, I shall recognize six fundamental principles:

(1) The projects should be useful.

(2) Projects shall be of a nature that a considerable proportion of the money spent will go into wages for labor.

(3) Projects will be sought which promise ultimate return to the Federal Treasury of a considerable proportion of the costs.

(4) Funds allotted for each project should be actually and promptly spent and not held over until later years.

(5) In all cases projects must be of a character to give employment to those on the relief rolls.

(6) Projects will be allocated to localities or relief areas in relation to the number of workers on relief rolls in those areas.

I next want to make it clear exactly how we shall direct the work.

(1) I have set up a Division of Applications and Information to which all proposals for the expenditure of money must go for preliminary study and consideration.

(2) After the Division of Applications and Information has sifted these projects, they will be sent to an Allotment Division composed of representatives of the more important governmental agencies charged with carrying on work relief projects. The group will also include representatives of cities, and of labor, farming, banking, and industry. This Allotment Division will consider all of the recommendations submitted to it and such projects as they approve will be next submitted to the President who under the Act is required to make final allocations.

(3) The next step will be to notify the proper Government agency in whose field the project falls, and also to notify another agency which I am creating—a Progress Division. This Division will have the duty of coordinating the purchase of materials and supplies and of making certain that people who are employed will be taken from the relief rolls. It will also have the responsibility of determining work payments in various localities, of making full use of existing employment services and of assisting people engaged in relief work to move as rapidly as possible back into private employment when such employment is available. Moreover, this Division will be charged with keeping projects moving on schedule.

(4) I have felt it to be essentially wise and prudent to avoid, so far as possible, the creation of new governmental machinery for supervising this work. The national Government now has at least sixty different agencies with the staff and the experience and the competence necessary to carry on the two hundred and fifty or three hundred kinds of work that will be undertaken. These agencies, therefore, will simply be doing on a somewhat enlarged scale, the same sort of things that they have been doing. This will make certain that the largest possible portion of the funds allotted will be spent for actually creating new work and not for building up expensive overhead organizations here in Washington.

For many months preparations have been under way. The allotment of funds for desirable projects has already begun. The key men for the major responsibilities of this great task already have been selected. I well realize that the country is expecting before this year is out to see the "dirt fly," as they say, in carrying on the work, and I assure my fellow citizens that no energy will be spared in using these funds effectively to make a major attack upon the problem of unemployment.

Our responsibility is to all of the people in this country. This is a great national crusade to destroy enforced idleness which is an enemy of the human spirit generated by this depression. Our attack upon these enemies must be without stint and without discrimination. No sectional, no political distinctions can be permitted.

It must, however, be recognized that when an enterprise of this character is extended over more than three thousand counties throughout the Nation, there may be occasional instances of inefficiency, bad management, or misuse of funds. When cases of this kind occur, there will be those, of course, who will try to tell you that the exceptional failure is characteristic of the entire endeavor. It should be remembered that in every big job there are some imperfections. There are chiselers in every walk of life, there are those in every industry who are guilty of unfair practices; every profession has its black sheep, but long experience in Government has taught me that the exceptional instances of wrongdoing in Government are probably less numerous than in almost every other line of endeavor. The most effective means of preventing such evils in this Works Relief program will be the eternal vigilance of the American people themselves. I call upon my fellow citizens everywhere to cooperate with me in making this the most efficient and the cleanest example of public enterprise the world has ever seen.

It is time to provide a smashing answer for those cynical men who say that a Democracy cannot be honest and efficient. If you will help, this can be done. I, therefore, hope you will watch the work in every corner of this Nation. Feel free to criticize. Tell me of instances where work can be done better, or where improper practices prevail. Neither you nor I want criticism conceived in a purely fault-finding or partisan spirit, but I am jealous of the right of every citizen to call to the attention of his or her Government examples of how the public money can be more effectively spent for the benefit of the American people....

Never since my Inauguration in March, 1933, have I felt so unmistakably the atmosphere of recovery. But it is more than the recovery of the material basis of our individual lives. It is the recovery of confidence in our democratic processes and institutions. We have survived all of the arduous burdens and the threatening dangers of a great economic calamity. We have in the darkest moments of our national trials retained our faith in our own ability to master our destiny. Fear is vanishing and confidence is growing on every side, faith is being renewed in the vast possibilities of human beings to improve their material and spiritual status through the instrumentality of the democratic form of government. That faith is receiving its just reward. For that we can be thankful to the God who watches over America.

Source

Roosevelt, Franklin D. "Fireside Chat, April 28, 1935." In *The Public Papers and Addresses of Franklin D. Roosevelt, Vol. 4: The Court Disapproves, 1935*. New York: Random House, 1938, pp. 133-38.

Residents of the Southern United States Recall the WPA

In his book Remembering the Great Depression in the Rural South, *Kenneth J. Bindas surveyed the experiences of residents of the American South during the 1930s. The following excerpt focuses on their impressions of the Works Progress Administration (WPA). According to Bindas, residents of the economically devastated small towns of the South tended to view the WPA as a positive force that played an essential role in helping them survive the hard times of the Depression.*

Most of the respondents recalled the WPA in much the same manner as they had the CCC [Civilian Conservation Corps]: a benefit to families, to communities, and to country. When Merrill Horton graduated from high school, he tried to get on the WPA but was refused because they told him there were "so many married men with families and children" who needed work. While disappointed, Horton understood that individual sacrifices were necessary for the country to emerge from the dark days of the Depression, and this was his small role in that process. Others retold stories of their own family situations, such as Clifford Oxford's unemployed pharmacist father. Thrown out of work by the Depression, he worked for nearly a year for the WPA. Oxford remembered that "it was the only paying job [his dad] could find in order for [the family] to survive and pay the rent." Clare Doherty's father faced similar problems after he lost his business. He first tried to get something else going by borrowing a wagon and selling vegetables, but after this venture failed, he joined the WPA. Although not used to hard labor, he learned how to lay brick and worked with the project building roads. He did not make a lot of money, Doherty recalled, "but he made enough that we didn't starve ... and [paid] out rent."

Many recalled how the WPA helped them more directly. Gladys H. Burroughs's husband worked on the WPA shortly after they married in 1935, "because, you know, in the country that was about all the jobs there were." Sarah Riddle's husband also worked for the WPA, helping to clear the way for building roads. He was not paid much, she recalled, but it was better than the wages he had received picking cotton—thirty cents for every one hundred pounds. Allan Furline remembered that his wages went from "making fifty cents a day to two dollars a day" building roads with the WPA. The fifty-cents-a-day wage must have been standard for unskilled white laborers, because many recalled

Kenneth J. Bindas, *Remembering the Great Depression in the Rural South.* Gainesville: University Press of Florida, 2007. Reprinted with permission of the University Press of Florida.

the same wage. Delmas Easterwood's husband worked with the WPA in Roanoke, Virginia, to "pour the streets of Roanoke" for "twenty-five cents an hour [which] was a great improvement over making fifty cents a day!" Making roads back then was a bit different than it is now, recalled Josephine Taff: "Tractors, and these big old things to work on the roads, they didn't have them. They worked [with] mules, picks and shovels." The work was not reserved for white workers, as Madie Myers recalled that around Columbus, Georgia, the WPA "gave men jobs, colored men." She was unsure whether white folks were part of the WPA or any government program: "I don't know if it was [just] in the black area but I know the WPA was something that had a lot of people working on it." E. LeRoy Jordan was one of those "colored men" in the area working on the WPA. He recalled getting on the WPA to help clear the land for building roads in and around Fort Benning, outside Columbus, Georgia. They only worked "one or two day[s] a week," and they had to bring their own tools. In Jordan's case, he brought a shovel.

Some recalled the WPA in a more personal manner. Geneva Stewart remembered that one time a "man and his wife [came] and stayed with us while her husband worked on that WPA" in Carrollton, Georgia. The wife stayed at the house and minded Stewart's children while she and her husband went to work in the textile mill. The couple "didn't pay no board" but lived there while he did work for the WPA. Naomi Jean Bowden's mother worked as a supervisor in a WPA sewing project, in which the "government gave them the cloth" and the clothing that they made was given to "whoever needed 'em." Sylvia Selman worked in a WPA nursery school in Rome, Georgia, so that the children's parents could work. "We gave them their lunch and they had a little cot to sleep on," she recalled, "and we gave them snacks before their mothers came for them." For her, the project signaled "hope" and that the government "would do something to help them."

Several stories came from those whose lives were changed by the WPA. Lillian Wrinkle grew up in the small town of Benton, Tennessee, with a dream of one day going to college. Graduating from high school in 1939, she spent the year looking for a way out of Benton, but with neither transportation nor opportunity, hope was dimming. "Finally the chance came" for her to travel the fifteen miles to Cleveland, Tennessee, as a neighbor who was a teacher at a local CCC camp offered to take her to Cleveland to sign up for the WPA. She worked as the teacher's aide in the camp, helping to teach the CCC boys to "read and write." When the camp disbanded, she left the program and signed on with the

National Youth Administration (NYA) to realize her dream of going "to business school." For William Gordon, a black man in central Georgia, the Depression meant that he worked for ten cents a day with meals and a place to stay. Gordon placed the blame on Hoover, saying the president made it so "poor people who depended on the white man, he keep you hungry so you could work a little more." Times were tough, but with FDR came food and a "work program, the WPA." Gordon made twenty dollars and ten cents every two weeks, he recalled, and he credited Roosevelt with being "the best president ... for the people."

Most of those interviewed viewed the WPA as a positive project that gave aid to folks who needed it and left behind a stronger nation. Stella Bowie said that the WPA projects in the area of Jacksonville, Florida, during the 1930s "gave men something to work for and have a little money and have a little dignity left." She believed that the terminal unemployment of the primary breadwinner in many families was detrimental not only to the recovery of the country but also to the people who made up the country. Even as the people saw the good in the WPA, however, they related jokes about the project. Young Lester of Atlanta said that the WPA "was the first time shovels had been invented with seats on them." Paul Maddox, also of Atlanta, told his interviewer about a terrible accident on a road the WPA was working on. It seemed that "termites ate up the handles on the shovels they were using" to lean on, causing the road-workers to fall and hurt themselves. James Harper said that some folks believed the WPA had more people than jobs, leading them to change the name to "We Piddle Around."

Maybe this perception was held more firmly by those in the cities, as few jokes or criticisms of the WPA came from informants from rural areas. Among these people, there was little criticism of the WPA or any New Deal program as being soft or coddling workers. Many agreed with Lizzie Johnson of Bowdon, Georgia, in her assessment of the project. In recalling her brother's WPA employment, she said, "Folks didn't have no jobs or nothing and he would work on the roads" with the WPA. The labor was hard, but the family appreciated his ability to bring home some money. Lois Scroggins of neighboring Villa Rica, Georgia, pointed to the community benefits of the program: "They built a swimming pool and a regular recreation place" for the people to use, which helped bring folks "out of the dumps." Tom Skelton worked at a service station in rural Carnseville, Georgia, that also served as the WPA morning headquarters. Around 4 a.m. every weekday, the crew assembled while attending to that area's roads. He talked to the men—some from his area but many others from all over

Georgia—and determined that without the WPA, "we would have fought among ourselves, because it had [gotten] to that point" of survival. He labeled those he met in the early morning as "good honest working people [who] were caught" in a cycle that trapped them in poverty. Without the WPA, Skeleton said, "they would have starved."

Source

Bindas, Kenneth J. *Remembering the Great Depression in the Rural South.* Gainesville: University Press of Florida, 2007, pp. 52-55.

Hallie Flanagan Describes Harry Hopkins's Ideas about Work Relief

In the summer of 1935, as the operations of the Works Progress Administration (WPA) were being organized, agency director Harry Hopkins selected Hallie Flanagan to oversee the Federal Theatre Project (FTP). In late July, the two officials embarked on a train trip to Iowa, where Flanagan's appointment was officially announced at the National Theatre Conference. Flanagan's account of the trip and of two speeches delivered by Hopkins in Iowa provides a candid glimpse of the director's views on work relief and government-subsidized art, as well as insights into Flanagan's own aspirations for the FTP.

Since Mr. Hopkins was anxious from the first to stress the fact that the government enterprise was to be national in scope, he decided that the logical place to announce my appointment was the National Theatre Conference to be held at Iowa City on the occasion of the laying of the cornerstone of Mr. Mabie's University Theatre [named for University of Iowa drama teacher E. C. Mabie]. On July 24, Mr. Hopkins telephoned me to meet him in Washington on the following day and go with him to Iowa City.

It was an exciting trip. Mr. Hopkins talked about everything—about engineering, about the building of airports, about the cities and countryside through which we were passing; but no matter what we started to talk about, it ended up with what was at that time the core and center of his thinking—the relationship of government to the individual. Hadn't our government always acknowledged direct responsibility to the people? Hadn't it given away the national domain in free land to veterans and other settlers? Hadn't it given away vast lands to railroad companies to help them build their systems? Hadn't the government spent fortunes on internal improvements, subsidizing the building of roads and canals, waterways, and harbors? Hadn't the government subsidized infant industries by a protective tariff? Hadn't the government also given away other intangible parts of the public domain, such as franchises to public utilities, the power to issue currency and create credit to banks, patent rights to inventors? In all of these ways, government enlarged industries, put men to work and increased buying power.

The new work program, Mr. Hopkins believed, would accomplish these same ends by giving of the nation's resources in wages to the unemployed, in return for which they would help build and improve America.

At every stop, there were newspapermen and cameramen and men with briefcases who got on for conferences. Almost all of these men seemed to have certain characteristics in common: they were young, thin, overworked-looking, and tremendously alive. I remember particularly Howard Hunter, who got on at Englewood to ride into Chicago.

"Can't I have peace even when the train's in motion?" said Mr. Hopkins. "What's on your mind? Can't you control Chicago?"

"I can control Chicago, all right," said Howard Hunter. He looked as if he could, too. "But I can't control Washington." He thumped his bulging briefcase. "See this? I've got questions that ought to have been answered six weeks ago. Seventy-five thousand people can't get paid until those questions are answered. And Washington sits back on its haunches and does absolutely nothing."

Hopkins grinned. "You're in control out here. What's the use of having a regional administrator if he can't administrate? And things are going to get more and more complicated because I'm setting up some art projects and they're going to be nationally directed and you boys are just going to love that."

Howard Hunter groaned and laughed and so did I, and that was the beginning of a good many groans and laughs we had together, including those over *Spirochete* and *The Swing Mikado*.

It was on this trip that Mr. Hopkins asked me a searching question. It is a question which is bound to be jeered at by critics of New Deal philosophy, but it is one of the questions at the core of that philosophy. The train through Chicago out to the midwest plains passed through the slums, and Mr. Hopkins, looking out over the abscessed gray tenements mercilessly exposed under the blinding sun, suddenly asked:

"Can you spend money?"

I said that inability to spend money was not one of my faults, but Mr. Hopkins continued seriously: "It's not easy. It takes a lot of nerve to put your signature down on a piece of paper when it means that the government of the United States is going to pay out a million dollars to the unemployed in Chicago. It takes decision, because you'll have to decide whether Chicago needs that money more than New York City or Los Angeles. You can't care very much what people are going to say because when you're handling other people's money whatever you do is always wrong. If you try to hold down wages, you'll be accused of union-busting and of grinding down the poor; if you pay a decent wage, you'll be competing with private industry and pampering a lot of no-accounts; if you scrimp on production costs, they'll say your shows are lousy and if you spend enough to get a good show on, they'll say you're wasting the taxpayers' money. Don't forget that whatever happens you'll be wrong."

With that reassuring preface, Mr. Hopkins launched into the reasons why, in spite of jeers, in spite of attacks, in spite of vituperation, we must spend money. These slums through which we were riding, these ramshackle, vermin-infested buildings housing our fellow citizens were one reason. These pale children sitting listlessly on fire-escapes were another. Sullen youths hanging around our street comers were another. Worried-looking men, gathered in silent knots before employment agencies, were still another. Houses for these people to live in, parks and playgrounds, fresh air, fresh milk and medical care for these children, schools and recreation places for youth to go to, jobs for men to do. Above all—jobs for men to do. *Danger: Men Not Working.* These were some of the reasons why we had to be able to spend money.

"It costs money to put a man to work and that's why a lot of people prefer direct relief. These people say that if we make the working conditions decent and give people a reasonable minimum to live on, people will get to like their jobs. They suggest that we make relief as degrading and shameful as possible so that people will want to get 'off.' Well—I've been dealing with unemployed people for years in one way and another and they *do* want to get off—but they can't, apparently, get 'off' into private industry. Well—if they can't get off into private industry where can they turn if they can't turn to their government? What's a government for? And these people can be useful to America; they can do jobs no one else can afford to—these slums, for instance. No private concern can afford to make houses for poor people to live in, because any private concern has got to show a profit. Why, we've got enough work to do right here in America, work that needs to be done and that no private concern can afford to touch, to lay out a program for twenty years and to employ every unemployed person in this country to carry out."

What part could art play in this program? Could we, through the power of the theatre, spotlight the tenements and thus help in the plan to build decent houses for all people? Could we through actors and artists who had themselves known privation, carry music and plays to children in city parks, and art galleries to little towns? Were not happy people at work the greatest bulwark of democracy?

That was Harry Hopkins' theme when he spoke the next night before a vast audience of farmers drawn from all over Iowa to the great campus of the State

University. He was the boy back in the home state and of course he played that up. He was never above a certain amount of hokum, and on that occasion he pulled a piece of business that would delight any stage manager. It was a hot night and the farmers were in their shirtsleeves. Harry painted the picture of poverty and desolation before work relief had come along, launched the work theme, built up a thrilling story of what it could do. He came to a climax and at that point someone in the crowd called out, "Who's going to pay for all that?"

That was the question they had been waiting for. On his answer everything depended. Would he hedge? He did not hedge. He looked out over the crowd. He took off his coat, unfastened his tie and took it off, rolled up his sleeves. The crowd got perfectly still. Then he said, "You are." His voice took on urgency. "And who better? Who can better afford to pay for it? Look at this great university. Look at these fields, these forests and rivers. This is America, the richest country in the world. We can afford to pay for anything we want. And we want a decent life for all the people in this country. And we are going to pay for it."

No more natural place for the announcement of a nationwide government theatre could be imagined than the National Theatre Conference at Iowa University, where people from all over the United States met for the laying of the cornerstone of an institution which was to be not only a civic and university theatre, but a regional center for the entire Midwest. After the ceremony we all went back to the hall of the Art Building where, after dinner, President Gilmore of the University introduced Elmer Rice, Paul Green, and other speakers. Harry Hopkins spoke of the new kind of theatre we hoped to create in America; he concluded with a fearless statement of policy: "I am asked whether a theatre subsidized by the government can be kept free from censorship, and I say, yes, it is going to be kept free from censorship. What we want is a free, adult, uncensored theatre."

I took this declaration seriously, as did my associates, and that is the kind of theatre we spent the next four years trying to build.

Source

Flanagan, Hallie. *Arena: The History of the Federal Theatre.* New York: Benjamin Brom, 1940, reissue 1965, pp. 24-29.

The WPA Explains Its Mission

This excerpt is taken from Our Job with the WPA, *a handbook provided to workers newly hired by the agency. In addition to answering frequently asked questions about issues such as pay, hours, and working conditions, the booklet devotes a number of pages to explaining the rationale behind the agency's operations. This section makes a case for why work relief is better than the dole, employing design elements that embody the distinctive style found in many WPA arts endeavors.*

« WE HAVE A WPA JOB »

It makes our work easier
to tackle when we know

« **Why we have a WPA job**

« **Why we have work
instead of a dole**

« **What good we are doing**

The principles underlying WPA are principles that have made America great **» » »**

HARD

WORK

AND

COMMON

SENSE

» 22 «

Let's see where we stand
with the rest of the workers:

At least a million former workers are unable to work because they are too old or
sick or otherwise unemployable.

Several millions more are unemployed but
have money or relatives or friends supporting them. They can get by for the present
without private jobs.

But there are other millions, most of them
with families or relatives they must help,
who have neither jobs nor help of any kind.
We belong to this group.

All the private jobs in the country are held
by the rest of America's workers.

Why can't we get private jobs?

» 23 «

189

Some of the reasons why we are still looking for private jobs

YOUNG MEN AND WOMEN JUST OUT OF SCHOOL MAKE MORE COMPETITION

BUSINESS HAS NOT YET FULLY RECOVERED

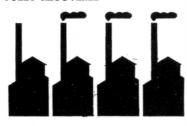

THE UNEMPLOYED NOT YET ON RELIEF GET THE JOBS FIRST

MACHINES TAKE OUR PLACES

These things
are beyond our control

This puts it up to Uncle Sam
to do something

Let's see what he can do

» 24 «

Uncle Sam Can:

LET US STARVE

NOT IN THIS MAN'S COUNTRY

GIVE US A DOLE

BUT WHO WANTS A HANDOUT?

LET US WORK

WHICH IS EVERY MAN'S RIGHT

The country will be richer if we build:

- « ROADS
- « SCHOOLS
- « AIRPORTS
- « SEWER SYSTEMS
- « WATER SYSTEMS
- « PARKS
- « PLAYGROUNDS
- « PUBLIC BUILDINGS
- « LIBRARIES
- « BETTER HEALTH

There are 3,000,000 of us:

- « TO DO THE WORK!
- « WE NEED THE WORK!
- « WE CAN DO THE WORK!

What's the answer?

Before we answer
let's look at the dole

» 25 «

What happens to us when we are on the dole

WE LOSE OUR SELF RESPECT

WE LOAF ON STREET CORNERS

WE LOSE OUR SKILL

FINALLY WE LOSE HOPE

WE HAVE FAMILY ROWS

Now let's look at what work does for us

» 26 «

192

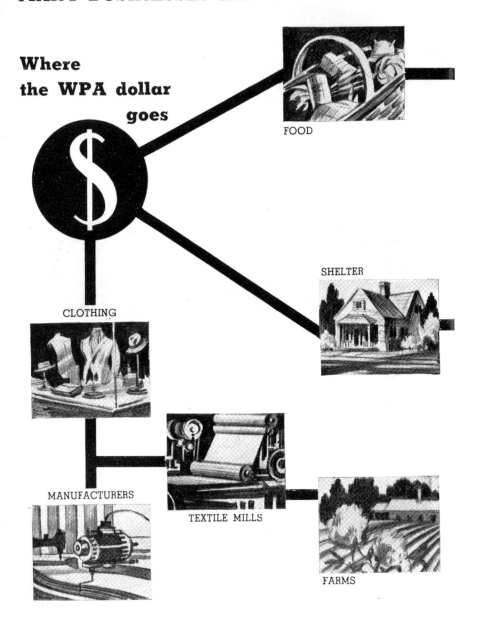

OUR WORKING AND SPENDING KEEP MANY BUSINESSES ALIVE

Where the WPA dollar goes

FOOD

SHELTER

CLOTHING

MANUFACTURERS

TEXTILE MILLS

FARMS

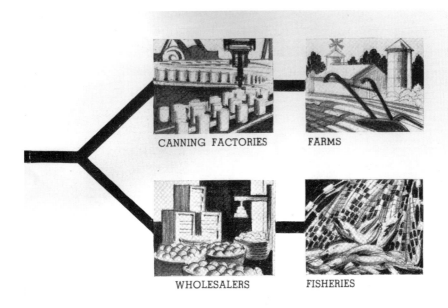

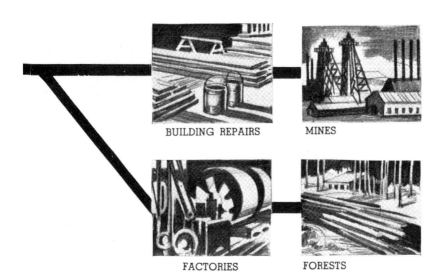

Work is the American Way

Source

Our Job with the WPA. Washington, DC: U.S. Government Printing Office, 1936.

A Young Artist Describes His Experiences with the WPA's Federal Art Project

Jacob Kainen was a young artist working to develop his talents in New York City when he joined the Graphic Arts Division of the Federal Art Project (FAP) of the Works Progress Administration (WPA) in the 1930s. In the following excerpt from his memoir about the project, he discusses positive aspects of the FAP as well as the many frustrating bureaucratic complications that had to be endured by work-relief artists. Kainen remained with the FAP, off and on, from 1935 to 1942. Though he was employed as a printmaker with the WPA, he was also an accomplished painter. He continued to work in both media after the Great Depression ended, eventually becoming an influential figure on the Washington, D.C., art scene.

There were times when working at the shop was particularly rewarding. On one occasion I was drawing on a stone when [well-known painter and graphic artist] Stuart Davis came by. I was twenty-six at the time. Inspired by his presence I made some bold decisions, almost reckless ones, that gave some verve and sparkle to the composition. It was probably the best print I made on the Project. I still remember with pleasure his kind words: "That's damn good." If more artists of Davis' caliber could have given us some personal attention, even if only to watch us work, I am sure we would have taken some unaccustomed chances and moved ahead in our art.

While work on the Project was exciting and stimulating, the hard facts of day-to-day relationships with the administration were generally unhappy. We realized that the Project administration was under pressure from its own administrative superiors, but that didn't alter the fact that we had to fight not only for reasonable working conditions but also for our economic existence. Political enemies and hostile critics, suspicious of cultural projects, made accusations of "boondoggling." In their zeal to obtain what they thought was full value for money received, they brought about regulations that were eminently in opposition to creative work. Most important among these were unrealistic supervisory methods, periodic firing of artists, and uncomprehending attitudes towards artistic creation.

In New York City, in the first years of the Project, an artist was required to go from his home each day to a central location and sign in by 9 a.m. He then

Reprinted from O'Connor, Francis V., ed. *The New Deal Art Projects: An Anthology of Memoirs*, Smithsonian Institution Press (1972), with permission of Smithsonian Institution.

returned home to work. This rule was not only wasteful of his time, it completely overlooked the fact that artists do not necessarily operate on a 9 to 5 schedule. One useful by-product of the signing-in practice was that it brought the artists together for a time to exchange pleasantries....

Artists were required to remain home at all times after registering in the morning. Periodically, timekeepers checked on them at unspecified hours. If the artist did not answer the door he was recorded as absent without leave. Consequently an artist hesitated to go out to get materials he needed, no matter how necessary, and even to visit the bathroom for fear the timekeeper might come during his absence.

If an artist wanted to go outside to sketch and gather subject material he had to notify the administration, giving the precise time when he could be found at a specified place. Often, a timekeeper was sent to make sure that the artist was on the spot. Naturally, this procedure wasted the artist's time and kept him from wandering about—the only way he could find unexpected subject matter. These timekeeping abuses, characteristic of the first few years, were later relaxed when it became evident to government officials, who dictated to the Project administration, that treating artists like factory hands was an unrealistic way to sponsor the production of works of art. If the administration bore the brunt of the artists' resentment it was because the artists had no way of knowing where the regulations came from and how and to what degree the administration resisted unreasonable orders from above.

Timekeeping methods were a nuisance and a bore but they were not the worst abuse the artist had to bear. Moreover they were eventually straightened out. The worst problem the artist had to face was the policy, begun in 1939, of firing Project members every eighteen months, ostensibly to allow them to look for private work. The policy was transparently fraudulent, since private jobs, especially for artists, did not exist. Actually the mass firings began as early as the fall of 1936. In July 1937 over seventy artists were dismissed with no advance notice. No apparent standards were followed in selecting artists for dismissal since those discharged included such prominent names as Joseph Stella, Julian Levi, Fritz Eichenberg, and Ben-Zion. Many in the group were noncitizens living in this country, including Chinese and Japanese who were specifically excluded from American citizenship by law at that time. Among those discharged was a large number of printmakers....

An artist could return to the Project, but the procedures for doing so were strenuous and demeaning. He had to declare himself a pauper and qualify for home relief. Then he had to wait in a home relief center every day of every week, sitting on a hard bench in a dreary waiting room together with other unemployed persons and homeless derelicts. He kept his eye on a blackboard, on which a clerk would occasionally list a job opening in white chalk. The artist remained there, if he was determined to get back on the Project, while such jobs as "dishwasher," "laborer," "porter," and the like were inscribed. When, finally, there appeared the words "graphic artist, WPA, 110 King Street," he made a mad dash for the exit and took the first street-car for his destination. It never occurred to us to take taxis; they were alien to our world and in any case we didn't have the money. The artist who got there first got the job....

It should be obvious to anyone that this sort of firing and hiring, in an economic depression, was frightening. It infected our thinking, consciously and unconsciously, and gave us the feeling of leading a transient existence. Certainly it created an uncertain and tentative atmosphere, one that was hardly conducive to the formation of a strong personal outlook, which must be built up in a careful and consecutive manner. This situation, in large measure, kept us from fully concentrating on our art and prevented us from expanding our possibilities naturally.

As one who joined the graphic arts division in its first month, I can testify to the enthusiasm and good will felt by participating artists. Aside from the relief at being able to survive economically, we were grateful to the government for recognizing that art was a public concern. It was good to know that we could function full-time as artists and work in a spirit of camaraderie with other artists and with master craftsmen. We had been given a strong professional motivation at a crucial time, and we appreciated it. One of the tragedies of the WPA/FAP was that the artists were treated as beggars by the relief-orientated policies of the WPA (not by Mrs. McMahon [Audrey McMahon—FAP regional director for the New York area] and her staff), their creative problems were not understood, and their work was grossly undervalued.

But the experience of producing prints and having them professionally printed was a constant pleasure and made up for the numerous indignities. It was in the shop that the printmakers felt most truly at home. There they could proof their blocks, plates, and stones in company with outstanding professionals such as Stuart Davis, Raphael Soyer, Yasuo Kuniyoshi, Adolf Dehn, Louis Lozowick, George Constant, and others. There was no "star" system—we were all in the same boat. We were stimulated by each other's presence and by the fact that productivity was a common requirement.

Source

Kainen, Jacob. "The Graphic Arts Division of the WPA Federal Art Project." In *The New Deal Art Projects: An Anthology of Memoirs,* edited by Francis V. O'Connor. Washington, DC: Smithsonian Institution Press, 1972, pp. 162-66.

An Actor in the Federal Theatre Project Recalls the Staging of *The Cradle Will Rock*

Hiram "Chubb" Sherman was one of the actors in the Federal Theatre Project company run by Orson Welles and John Houseman during the mid-1930s. After the Depression ended, Sherman went on to enjoy a long career as a stage, television, and film actor. In the following excerpt from Hard Times *by Studs Terkel, Sherman discusses his experiences with the company and recalls the controversial musical* The Cradle Will Rock, *which was staged in 1937 even after its opening had been prohibited by WPA officials.*

In 1936, I joined the Federal Theater. I was assigned to Project 891. The directors and producers were Orson Welles and John Houseman. The theater we had taken over was the Maxine Elliott. A lot of theaters went dark during the Depression, and the theater owners were happy to lease them to the Government.

One of the marvelous things about the Federal Theater, it wasn't bound by commercial standards. It could take on poetic drama and do it. And experimental theater. The Living Newspaper made for terribly exciting productions. Yet it was theater by bureaucracy. Everything had to go to a higher authority. There were endless chits to be approved. There were comic and wasteful moments all over the country. But it was forward-thinking in so many ways. It anticipated some of today's problems. The Unit I was in was integrated. We did Marlowe's *Doctor Faustus*. Mephistopheles was played by a Negro, Jack Carter. Orson Welles played Faustus.

Our next production was *Cradle Will Rock*, words and music by Marc Blitzstein. And we rehearsed those eight hours a day. We worked every moment, and sometimes we worked overtime because we loved it.

Cradle Will Rock was for its day a revolutionary piece. It was an attack on big business and the corruption involved. It was done *à la* [German playwright Bertolt] Brecht. We had it fully rehearsed.

On opening night, when the audience was assembling in the street, we found the doors of the Maxine Elliott closed. They wouldn't admit the audience because of an edict from Washington that this was revolutionary fare. And we would have no performance. Somebody had sent down the word.

Well, when you have an alert company, who are all keyed up at this moment, and a master of publicity such as Orson Welles, this is just grist for their mills. (Laughs.)

It's a nice evening in May—late May or April. Balmy evening. An audience not able to get into a theater, but not leaving because the directors of 891, Orson Welles and John Houseman, were haranguing them in the street: "Don't leave!" They expected to get a reversal of the edict. We're told not to make up. We're told not to go home. We don't know what's going to happen.

No reversal came from Washington. So Orson and John Houseman got their friends on the phone: What theater could we do this in? Somebody suggested the Jolson Theater. An announcement was made to all these people, without benefit of microphone: if you go to the Jolson Theater you will see the show. And we marched. Walking with our audience around into Broadway and then up Seventh Avenue to Fifty-ninth Street, we acquired an even larger audience.

Walking down the middle of the street?

Oh yes. Walking with no police permit. (Laughs.) Just overflowing the sidewalks. Obviously something was afoot. The Jolson Theater hadn't had a booking for months and was very dusty. But it was open.

Word came from Actors Equity that proper bonding arrangements had not been made. The actors would not be allowed to appear on the stage. Because now you're not under the aegis [protection] of the Federal Theater. You're under some obscure private management. You don't know what, because you haven't found out yet.

This didn't daunt us. We had a colloquy [discussion] right in the alley. We decided, well, if we can't go on the stage, we could wheel out the piano and Marc Blitzstein could do what he had done in so many auditions: describe the setting and such, and we'll all sit in the audience. Equity didn't say we couldn't sit in the audience. When our cues come, we will rise and give them. So, that we did.

The theater filled. I don't know how the extra people, who didn't hold tickets for the opening, how they got in. I've often wondered. Did the box office open or did they just say: come in for the laughs? But it was packed with people. The stage was bare, the curtain was up, and you suddenly missed all your fellow actors. You couldn't find them. We were in different parts of the house.

Eventually the house lights lowered a little. Marc Blitzstein came out and laid the setting and played a few bars and then said: "Enter the whore." I didn't know where Olive Stanton, who played the whore, was. Suddenly you could hear Olive's very clear high voice, from over left. A spotlight suddenly found her and she stood up. She was in the lower left-hand box. One by one, as we were called up, we joined in. We turned around if we were down front, and faced the audience. People were scattered all over. It was a most exciting evening. The audience reaction was tremendous.

One of those summers, '38, '39, I don't know which—Marc Blitzstein corraled most of us who'd been in the original company and asked us if we'd give up Sunday to go give a performance of *Cradle Will Rock* in Bethlehem, Pennsylvania. I thought this was marvelous. Because we're now going to take *Cradle Will Rock* to the workers, to the people for whom he wrote this piece. We were all corraled into a bus and off we went on a nice, hot summer's day. I thought, well, pretty soon the mills will close down and the steel workers will pour into this amusement park, as twilight comes, and they'll hear this marvelous saga. No one showed up.

A few men drifted in, and the first thing you find out is that many of them do not understand or speak English. And this was written in, supposedly, common American speech. Here we were an opera for the proletariat, and the proletariat neither wants nor understands it. It's a rather shocking occurrence. But you don't give up.

You're in a hot, sort of open auditorium. And Will Geer, never to be discouraged, [was] scrounging around for an audience. He found a picnic of church ladies over an adjoining hill. They were spreading out their picnic baskets and he asked: "Would you like to be entertained with an opera?" They allowed as how they would, and they packed their gingham table cloths, all the sandwiches and brought them over to this little amusement place. And sat down.

Marc Blitzstein came out and announced the name of this piece was *Cradle Will Rock*, the setting was Steeltown, U.S.A., and it begins on a street corner at night, and enter the whore. When he said those words, our audience got up and packed up their picnic baskets and left us. We never did *Cradle Will Rock* in Bethlehem, Pennsylvania.

Source

"Hiram (Chubb) Sherman." In Terkel, Studs. *Hard Times: An Oral History of the Great Depression.* New York: New Press, 2005, pp. 364-67. First published in 1970 by Pantheon Books.

The FTP's "Living Newspaper" Plays—Insightful Commentary or Government Propaganda?

The "Living Newspaper" plays produced by the Federal Theatre Project were among the most provocative and controversial works created by the Works Progress Administration arts programs. Power, a play written by Arthur Arent that first opened in New York in March 1937, followed the pattern of other Living Newspaper productions: it examined a current news topic—in this case, the efforts of the Tennessee Valley Authority (TVA) to build hydroelectric dams and other infrastructure that provided affordable electricity to rural areas of the southeastern United States—in the form of a play. The following excerpt from Power refers to the use of film footage in the performance, an innovation that often figured in Living Newspaper dramas. This excerpt, however, also illustrates why opponents of the New Deal criticized these works. The play's positive portrayal of the TVA, an agency created under the Roosevelt administration, led to charges that the drama was being used as a political tool to promote the president and his policies.

SCENE FIFTEEN—C

(Farmer and Electric Company Manager)

(*Lights come up on desk.* MANAGER *of Electric Company is seated at desk.* FARMER, *left of desk, stands.*)

FARMER: [Fictional character.] My God, I've got to have lights, I tell you!

MANAGER: [*Ibid.*] Certainly, Mr. Parker. You can have all the lights you want. All you've got to do is pay for the cost of poles and wires.

FARMER: But I haven't got four hundred dollars! And my farm's mortgaged up to the hilt already. (*Desperately*) Can't you see? If I could only get juice I could get me an electric churn and make enough money to pay for the poles!

MANAGER: I'm sorry, Mr. Parker, but that's the way we operate. I'm afraid I can't do a thing for you.

FARMER: And I got to go on livin' the rest of my life with a kerosene lamp and a hand churn like my grandfather did when he came here?

MANAGER: Until you can raise the cost of the equipment.

FARMER: (*desperately*): Isn't there anybody else I can talk to?

MANAGER: I'm the manager here. There's nobody else.

FARMER: Isn't there any other company I can go to?

MANAGER: We're the only one in this part of the State.

FARMER: Then when you turn me down I'm finished?

MANAGER: That's right. (A *pause*.)

FARMER: By God, the Government ought to do something about this!

Blackout

SCENE FIFTEEN—D

(City Man and Commissioner)

(*Lights up on desk.* COMMISSIONER *seated,* MAN *standing, right of desk.*)

MAN: [Fictional character.] Mr. Commissioner, my electric bills are too high!

COMMISSIONER: [*Ibid.*] Have you had your meter tested?

MAN: Yes, I've had it tested twice. The meter's all right, but the bills are too high just the same.

COMMISSIONER: Mr. Clark, you're not paying one cent more for your electricity than anybody else.

MAN: I know that! That's what the trouble is, we're *all* paying too much!

COMMISSIONER: Mr. Clark, the company that sells you is working on a margin of seven to eight per cent. We consider that a fair profit. And so will you, if you're a business man.

MAN: Look, Mr. Commissioner. I'm not asking you to argue with me on behalf of the utilities. I am a taxpayer! I'm paying your salary. I want you to go and argue with them! What's the Commission for, if it's not to help guys like me?

COMMISSIONER: Mr. Clark, the law permits any private enterprise to make a fair return on its investment.

MAN: It does, eh?

COMMISSIONER: And the law permits any company to charge any rate so long as that fair profit is maintained.

MAN: It does, eh? Well, tell me this: If laws like that are made for utilities, why aren't laws made to help people like me?

(*General lighting on entire stage reveals* FARMER, *his* WIFE, *and* CITY WIFE *in their former positions.*)

205

FARMER'S WIFE: *And me!*

CITY WIFE: *And me!*

FARMER: *And me!*

Blackout

SCENE FIFTEEN—E

(Parade and TVA Song)

LOUDSPEAKER: May 18th, 1933. The United States Government answers. [**New York Times, May 19, 1933.**]

(Lights pick up **CLERK** *of Senate.)*

CLERK *(reads)*: The Tennessee Valley Authority is created for the purpose of: one, flood control of the Tennessee River Basin; two, elimination of soil erosion, and three, the social and economic rehabilitation of the swampland and hill people of this district; four, the generation and distribution of cheap electric power and the establishment of a cost yardstick. (*As the* **CLERK** *reaches the words "the social and economic rehabilitation" orchestra plays the TVA song very softly. When the* **CLERK** *reaches the words "cost yardstick" lights fade on him. A motion picture of TVA activities and water flowing over the Norris Dam appears on the scrim [a type of theatre screen], and through the scrim and on projection curtain upstage. A parade of men and women comes on stage behind scrim, singing the TVA song. Many of them carry lanterns. Red, yellow and amber side lights pick up the parade. They circle the stage and continue the song until act curtain falls, which comes down on movie of second large waterfall.*)

THE TVA SONG:
[Used with permission of copyright owner, Jean Thomas.]

My name is William Edwards,
       I live down Cove Creek Way;
I'm working on the project
       They call the TVA.

The Government begun it
       When I was but a child,
And now they are in earnest
       And Tennessee's gone wild.

All up and down the valley
> They heard the glad alarm;
The Government means business—
> It's working like a charm.

Oh, see them boys a-comin',
> Their Government they trust,
Just hear their hammers ringin',
> They'll build that dam or bust!

For things are surely movin',
> Down here in Tennessee;
Good times for all the Valley,
> For Sally and for me.

Curtain

Movie continues on front curtain until end of film.

Source

Arent, Arthur. "Power: A Living Newspaper." In *Federal Theatre Plays*, edited by Pierre De Rohan. New York: Random House, 1938, pp. 66-69.

Herbert Hoover Condemns the Works Progress Administration

After being defeated by Franklin Roosevelt in the 1932 presidential election, former president Her-
bert Hoover became an outspoken critic of the New Deal. In the following excerpt from a speech
he delivered in September 1938, he contends that the relief efforts of the Roosevelt administration,
and particularly those carried out by the Works Progress Administration (WPA), are harming the
nation's moral and political foundations. Among other charges, Hoover argues that the WPA is being
used as a tool to improperly influence elections and that the agency's work-relief jobs are feeding
the growth of unethical "political machines" in a number of cities. He even compares WPA offi-
cials and political supporters to the Praetorian Guard, the military bodyguards who protected
ancient Roman emperors. Hoover also criticizes President Roosevelt and WPA officials Harry Hop-
kins and Aubrey Williams by name for condoning the agency's involvement in political affairs.

I n 1930 as President I announced that as a nation we "must prevent hunger
and cold to those of our people who are in honest difficulties." And I
undertook the organization of their relief. I had had some years' experience
elsewhere with the moral and political dangers in relief. I determined that America should not be subjected to those calamities. To prevent this we saw to it that
non-partisan committees of leading citizens were established in some 3,000
communities, where relief was needed. These committees were given the full
responsibility of administration. These committees were unpaid. They had no
vested interest in keeping unemployment going. At the start their money support was local. As the situation deepened, first the States and finally the Federal government gave financial aid to these committees. Parallel with this, we
greatly expanded useful Public Works at regular pay and full-time employment.

At this point I may wipe away a current New Deal crocodile tear. And that
wells constantly out of their emotion that they were the first Administration
with human sympathy or to give real relief to the distressed. They admit now
that when they took over the government in 1933, our relief organization was
regularly providing for over 5,400,000 distressed homes of over 21,000,000 persons. And these figures did not include Federal Public Works, nor the special
service to 400,000 veterans. What the New Deal in fact did was to wreck this
system of local, non-partisan administration and substitute a political administration centralized in Washington. After six years the practical relief situation

---

instead of being better is worse. The moral consequences have been degrading to the whole people.

Under local administration there was a summoning of community sympathy, a desire to help not alone with relief but with jobs and with encouragement. Today instead of being viewed as unfortunate and entitled to aid these Americans are being unjustly ridiculed as lazy parasites. But worse than even this, great numbers of self-reliant people are being inexorably moulded into the hopelessness of a permanent army of relief. A hierarchy of officials is being built whose jobs depend on keeping people on relief. And American youth is being poured into this mould. It is sheer madness. A class wall of hate and fear of those on relief is growing daily.

And now, national sympathy is being defiled by politics. Harry Hopkins and Aubrey Williams handle billions of your money given for relief of these distressed people. Messrs. Hopkins and Williams have the power in this Republic to say who shall have bread and who shall not.

You will recollect the trick words by which these men this last June effectually told people on relief how to vote—or else.

Ripped of all disguises and all intellectual dishonesty, the statements of these men were a direction to these millions and their wives and relatives how to vote.

The New Deal Senatorial Committee whitewashed those trick statements as inoffensive. Messrs. Hopkins and Williams know the millions of WPA workers understand the English language even if these Senators do not.

Even if these gentlemen had never made these remarks there is scarcely one of the thousands of appointees that direct the WPA who was selected under the non-partisan Civil Service. They were selected with the approval—or something stronger—of some Democratic County Chairman, some New Deal Congressman, or some other political person. It was in fact entirely superfluous for Messrs. Hopkins and Williams to have uttered a hint. These politicians will do the hinting to those distressed people anyway.

And the commanders of this detachment of the Praetorian Guard are even bolder. In the few months just prior to the 1934 Congressional election and the 1936 Presidential election, the business situation was improving. There was much less need for relief. A Congressional Committee has shown that nevertheless in those election months the number of people assisted by relief was greatly expanded. It also showed that in the same months in the off years they were greatly decreased. This was said to be a coincidence.

Again we approach an election. Again the business situation is improving and private jobs are increasing. But again more voters are being put on relief. No doubt this is also a coincidence.

If we want proof of this use of relief for pressure on the votes of distressed peoples we may turn to the recent record. The hideous morals of these actions in a free Republic were denounced by a few Democratic Senators whose morals rise above elections. Democratic Senator [Carl] Hatch proposed a law in the Senate designed to stop relief officials from using relief for vote-getting purposes. The Senator said, "Those who believe that out in the counties and in the cities and in the precincts this instrumentality which we have set up is not being used for political purposes are more credulous than I am."

However, Senator [Alben W.] Barkley, President Roosevelt's selected leader of the Senate, led the opposition to Senator Hatch's motion. The motion was defeated by President Roosevelt's rubber-stamp followers in the Senate.

Would this law have been defeated if President Roosevelt had breathed one whisper of approval for it? Or better, if he had expressed one word of indignation at the action of his supporters in the Senate? Instead, Mr. Roosevelt journeyed to Kentucky to endorse the re-election of Senator Barkley.

And this sample in Kentucky could not be unknown to Mr. Roosevelt. Some months ago the Democratic Scripps-Howard papers courageously exposed the use of the WPA in Kentucky "as a grand political racket in which the taxpayer is the victim." Harry Hopkins as usual denounced the reporter as untruthful. Later on, even the Senate Committee, after investigation, had to stigmatize this stench. They said, "These facts should arouse the conscience of the country. They imperil the right of the people to a free and unpolluted ballot." I notice it was the conscience of the country that they summoned. They apparently did not think it worth while to call it to the conscience of the President.

Mr. Roosevelt has mastered the power to bestow bread and butter to millions of people or withhold it from them. He called upon the people specifically in Kentucky, in Oklahoma, Georgia, South Carolina, and Maryland to vote for his selections for the Senate. At about the same time relief wages in those territories were raised. Mr. Roosevelt threw in a few bridges and announced a new economic program for the South by government subsidy. I may not believe all this has any connection with these primaries or this election. But the question is, Do the relief workers believe it? Of course the people on relief are free to vote the Republican ticket also. But do they know that?

Nor is this use of bait sectional. It envelops the whole nation. This spring when economic improvement was obvious without artificial stimulants and just before this election, this three-billion-dollar pump-priming program was enacted. The headlines daily flame with the assignment of some pork to every Congressional district. New Deal candidates proudly announce its arrival to their constituents. Cities and communities push in Washington to get their feet in the trough. Hundreds of them justify their manners at the Treasury by the immoral excuse that somebody else will get it. They organize a lobby to see they get it. And, worse still, government officials urge them to arrive early before the trough is empty.

Do you wonder that the whole world stands amazed at this supposedly great republic of free men? Do you wonder that every dictator in Europe uses this exhibit to prove the failure of self-government?

And there are still more ramifications of all this. Some of our local political organizations, whether Republican or Democratic, have not been perfect in the past. But we are today confronted with more disheartening growth of high-powered political machines in our cities than ever before in our history. Kansas City, Saint Louis, Jersey City, Philadelphia, Pittsburgh, Memphis, Chicago, and what not. It may be coincidence that these machines are supporting the New Deal. It is no coincidence that for six years the patronage and the subsidies of the New Deal have been handled by these political bosses.

We hear much Presidential urging of economic royalists to virtue. It is probably coincidence that we hear no moral urging of political royalists.

And these are but a few of the black spots. What of the stench of the primaries in Pennsylvania, New Mexico, Indiana and Tennessee? What of the indictments of high officials in Connecticut? In New York? What of the New Deal Governor of Pennsylvania who compels a legislature to suppress a Grand jury inquiry into charges of corruption against him?

And you know and I know that moral corruption by expenditure of these huge sums of public money penetrates every county and every village. The indignant citizen used to roll up his sleeves and with his neighbors hope to clean corruption in his own town. But when it floods from Washington what hope has he to stem the tide?

Do you wonder that our own people lose faith in honesty? Do they not lose faith in democracy? Does it not disintegrate the moral standards of our people?

This gigantic expenditure of public money will make its beneficiaries drunk on the basest selfishness and it will make any group drunk with power.

That seems to be one of the attractions of this New Deal Liberal Party.

Source

Hoover, Herbert. "Morals in Government." Address to Joint Republican Organizations, Kansas City, MO, September 28, 1938." In *Further Addresses Upon the American Road, 1938-1940*. New York: Scribner and Sons, 1940, pp. 3-20.

President Roosevelt Discontinues the WPA

As the economy gained strength in the early 1940s, the federal government dramatically reduced operations of the Work Projects Administration (originally called the Works Progress Administration). By 1942 the national unemployment rate had fallen below 5 percent and the work relief program was deemed no longer necessary. On December 4, 1942, President Franklin D. Roosevelt wrote the following letter to the Federal Works administrator announcing his plan to discontinue the agency, which he praised as a resounding success.

In my annual Message to the Congress seven years ago I outlined the principles of a Federal work relief program. The Work Projects Administration was established in May, 1935, and it has followed these basic principles through the years. This Government accepted the responsibility of providing useful employment for those who were able and willing to work but who could find no opportunities in private industry.

Seven years ago I was convinced that providing useful work is superior to any and every kind of dole. Experience has amply justified this policy.

By building airports, schools, highways, and parks; by making huge quantities of clothing for the unfortunate; by serving millions of lunches to school children; by almost immeasurable kinds and quantities of service the Work Projects Administration has reached a creative hand into every county in this Nation. It has added to the national wealth, has repaired the wastage of depression, and has strengthened the country to bear the burden of war. By employing eight millions of Americans, with thirty millions of dependents, it has brought to these people renewed hope and courage. It has maintained and increased their working skills; and it has enabled them once more to take their rightful places in public or in private employment.

Every employable American should be employed at prevailing wages in war industries, on farms, or in other private or public employment. The Work Projects Administration rolls have greatly decreased, through the tremendous increase in private employment, assisted by the training and reemployment efforts of its own organization, to a point where a national work relief program is no longer necessary. Certain groups of workers still remain on the rolls who may have to be given assistance by the States and localities; others will be able to find work on farms or in industry at prevailing rates of pay as private employment continues to increase. Some of the present certified war projects may have to be taken over by other units of the Federal Works Agency or by other departments of the Federal Government. State or local projects should be closed out by completing useful units of such projects or by arranging for the sponsors to carry on the work.

With these considerations in mind, I agree that you should direct the prompt liquidation of the affairs of the Work Projects Administration, thereby conserving a large amount of the funds appropriated to this organization. This will necessitate closing out all project operations in many States by February 1, 1943, and in other States as soon thereafter as feasible. By taking this action there will be no need to provide project funds for the Work Projects Administration in the budget for the next fiscal year.

I am proud of the Work Projects Administration organization. It has displayed courage and determination in the face of uninformed criticism. The knowledge and experience of this organization will be of great assistance in the consideration of a well-rounded public works program for the postwar period.

With the satisfaction of a good job well done and with a high sense of integrity, the Work Projects Administration has asked for and earned an honorable discharge.

Source

Roosevelt, Franklin D. "Letter to Federal Works Administrator, December 4, 1942." *The Public Papers and Addresses of Franklin D. Roosevelt, 1942 volume: Humanity on the Defensive.* New York: Harper & Brothers, 1950, p. 505-6.

Comparing the American Recovery and Reinvestment Act of 2009 to the WPA

When President Barack Obama took office in January 2009, one of his top priorities was to combat widespread unemployment. This high level of unemployment was the result of a severe economic recession that had taken root across the country the previous year. His administration's primary response to the recession was to craft the American Recovery and Reinvestment Act, which became law just one month after his inauguration. In the introduction to his book Money Well Spent, *which provides a detailed analysis of the act, journalist Michael Grabell compares the American Recovery and Reinvestment Act to the operations of the Works Progress Administration during the Great Depression.*

The American Recovery and Reinvestment Act was the largest economic recovery plan in history. Better known as "the stimulus," the $825 billion package passed in February 2009 included a mixture of tax cuts, safety net spending, and long-term investments in renewable energy, education, and infrastructures. Adjusted for inflation, it was nearly five times more expensive than the Works Progress Administration (WPA), credited with easing if not helping to end the Great Depression. The stimulus cost more than it did to fight the Iraq War from 2003 to 2010. It was bigger than the Louisiana Purchase, the Manhattan Project, the moon race, and the Marshall Plan to rebuild Europe after World War ll. When the various extensions of stimulus provisions are taken into account, the recovery program cost well over a trillion dollars....

The stimulus was designed in three parts. First, a flood of money in tax cuts, food stamps, and unemployment checks would get consumers spending. An even greater deluge of education and health care money would stop the bleeding in state budgets. Then, a wave of "shovel-ready" infrastructure projects would kick in, creating new jobs repaving roads and making homes more energy efficient. As the economy got churning again, new investments in wind farms, solar panel factories, electric cars, broadband, and high-speed rail would lead America out of the recession and into a twenty-first-century economy competitive with the rest of the world.

But it didn't happen like that. The White House's economists, like nearly every forecaster, misread the recession. The state assistance wasn't enough to plug the budget holes and, in many cases, the school aid merely delayed rather than prevented teacher layoffs. Infrastructure projects took months longer to break ground than the public had been led to believe. Such recovery as there was seemed weak, and investments in new technologies were decades away from rebuilding a manufacturing base for working Americans.

With these disappointments, the stimulus left a lasting impression on politics. Already seething from the bank bailout, the rush of public spending pushed small-government supporters over the edge, leading to Tea Party protests across the country. The early activism allowed like-minded people to find each other, organize the tax-day rallies, and coalesce into a movement that acquired more momentum as it confronted the health care reform bill in the summer and fall of 2009. In the midterm elections, Republican and Democratic shoo-ins became pariahs. Suddenly, the time-honored distinction of bringing money back to the home district became a liability. And an era of federal spending on America's greatest challenges seemed to come to an end.

A common theme in the news coverage was that the White House bungled the message on the stimulus. This is partly true. The emphasis on shovel-ready infrastructure inspired visions of the New Deal and created the impression that the stimulus was largely a public works package. It wasn't. But the administration spent little time showing off the areas where more money was spent: the teacher whose job was saved, the middle-class family whose taxes were cut. Since the stimulus passed, Obama administration officials have gone on more than four hundred trips to attend groundbreaking, announce funding, and otherwise promote the stimulus. Each time, they told the story of a president who put Americans to work, pulled the country back from the brink, and invested in the future. The Obama team had a far better narrative, but the Republicans had better talking points. And in a world where more and more Americans got their news in 140-character chunks and in the extremes of cable TV and blogs, the story didn't matter. It was the uppercut that counted.

The bigger problem was that so much of the stimulus was invisible. More than half of the package was in tax cuts and safety net programs. The largest single item in the Recovery Act was a $116 billion tax credit for the middle class. Rather than handing out checks, the economic team felt people were more likely to spend it if they didn't notice it. So instead, it was spread out in paychecks at about $10 a week. It worked. People didn't notice it. It was also difficult to imagine the world that might have been if there had been no stimulus. If a teacher was in the classroom, no one gave the administration any credit. Money for Medicaid, unemployment checks, and food stamps meant that somewhere down the line, a nurse and a grocery clerk kept their jobs. But it was hard to see the connection.

Of the parts that were visible, it often seemed that the stimulus was providing money for everything. Instead of investing in a few marquee projects, Congress tried to make the stimulus a cure-all. There was money for every one of society's ills, from cancer to cogon grass, from ailing infrastructure like bridges and rails to invasive species like Asian carp and Russian olive trees.

Critics seized upon the stimulus for silly-sounding projects: turtle tunnels, electric fish displays, and research involving monkeys and cocaine. But Earl Devaney, the burly inspector general brought in to investigate the stimulus, told me that ultimately very little of the money was lost to fraud, waste, and abuse.

In reading about the New Deal, I couldn't help but notice the similarities. Lost to the popular myth is the fact that the WPA was feverishly mocked during its day. Critics said the initials stood for "We Piddle Around." Louis Armstrong recorded a song called "WPA" with lines that went "Sleep while you work rest while you play / Lean on your shovel to pass the time away." One of the many jokes at the time told the story of a man whose brother had been trying to get into the WPA.

"What's he doing now?" another man asked.

"Nothing," he said. "He got the job."

The right wing at the time called the WPA a breeding ground for socialism and at a hearing on the Federal Emergency Relief Administration in 1935, a crafts instructor told of teaching men how to make "boon doggles," giving birth to the word applied to many stimulus projects today.

The New Deal has been glorified over time. As the story goes, Franklin D. Roosevelt put the down-and-out to work building enduring feats of engineering like the Hoover Dam and brought about an end to the Depression. In truth, it took four years for the unemployment rate, which peaked at 25 percent in 1933, to come down to 14 percent. It didn't return to normal until after World War II. The Hoover Dam took five years to build after taking more than two years to break ground. The project was actually authorized by Congress in 1928, before the stock market crash, during the administration of President Calvin Coolidge. It was constructed by the Bureau of Reclamation and the Public

Works Administration, not the WPA. While the WPA had its wonders, New York's LaGuardia Airport and San Francisco's Cow Palace among them, most of its projects were minor jobs building monuments, painting murals and paving roads.

What has changed is the scale of government. In building a modern system, we have developed a process and procedure for everything. Construction projects can't simply be doled out to untrained workers and begun tomorrow. To protect taxpayers, we've developed a process of competitive bidding, whereby any qualified contractor is given a fair shot to win the project. We've enacted environmental rules to ensure a project doesn't pollute streams or kill off wildlife. The U.S. Department of Transportation funds highway projects through a formula, in which the federal government picks up 80 percent of the cost. The Department of Education contributes billions of dollars every year for special education and disadvantaged students.

When measured as a percentage of the federal budget, the Recovery Act equaled a little more than 25 percent of the $3 trillion in regular government spending in 2009, including Social Security and Medicare. In contrast, the Public Works Administration, which cost $3.3 billion, was more than 70 percent of the federal budget in 1933. The $11 billion for the WPA was more than what the government typically spent in three years. In today's terms, it would be as if Congress passed a $2 trillion stimulus package in 2009 and followed up with another one worth $8 trillion a few years later. So while the New Deal probably felt like going from zero to sixty miles per hour, the Recovery Act was more like going from thirty-five to fifty.

Source

Grabell, Michael. *Money Well Spent?: The Truth behind the Trillion-Dollar Stimulus, the Biggest Economic Recovery Plan in History.* New York: Public Affairs, 2012, pp. ix-xiv.

IMPORTANT PEOPLE, PLACES, AND TERMS

Advisory Committee on Allotments
A federal government group that reviewed and approved the work projects undertaken by the Works Progress Administration and other agencies.

Bethune, Mary McLeod (1875-1955)
Director of the Office of Negro Affairs for the National Youth Administration.

Boondoggle
A term coined during the Great Depression to refer to a misguided government-sponsored task or program that has little value.

Cahill, Holger "Eddie" (1887-1960)
Director of the Federal Art Project of the Works Progress Administration.

CCC
See Civilian Conservation Corps (CCC).

Civil Works Administration (CWA)
New Deal agency that conducted a massive but short-lived work relief program from November 1933 through March 1934.

Civilian Conservation Corps (CCC)
A New Deal agency that operated from 1933 to 1942 to provide employment to young men between the ages of eighteen and twenty-five, primarily on conservation projects located in publicly owned wilderness areas.

Communism
An extreme form of socialism that abolishes all private ownership of property and resources, provides equal access to goods and services to all individuals, and generally calls for the revolutionary overthrow of capitalist systems.

Coughlin, Charles (1891-1979)
Catholic priest and radio broadcaster who became well known for his outspoken criticism of the New Deal and for his anti-Semitic views.

Court-packing plan
President Franklin Roosevelt's unsuccessful 1937 effort to reform the U.S. judicial system and increase the number of justices on the U.S. Supreme Court.

CWA
See Civil Works Administration (CWA).

Dies, Martin, Jr. (1900-1972)
U.S. representative from Texas who targeted alleged communist activity in the arts programs of the Works Progress Administration in his role as chair of the House Un-American Activities Committee.

Direct relief
A form of public assistance that provides those in need with money, goods, or services without requiring them to perform any work in return.

Dole, The
A negative term for direct relief—public assistance in which the recipients do not perform any type of work in return for the money, goods, or services that they are provided.

Emergency Relief Appropriation Acts
A series of laws that provided the authority and funding for the Works Progress Administration as well as other federal relief efforts. The initial law governing the WPA was the Emergency Relief Appropriation Act of 1935. Subsequent laws instituted changes in the agency's operations, particularly the Emergency Relief Appropriation Act of 1939, which mandated a number of reforms advocated by opponents of the New Deal.

FAP
See Federal Art Project (FAP).

Farm Security Administration (FSA)
A New Deal agency that assisted struggling farmers. Photographers hired by the FSA to document the experiences of rural Americans produced many of the iconic images of the Great Depression.

Federal Art Project (FAP)

A Works Progress Administration program that employed artists to produce painting, graphics, and sculpture and to teach art classes. The FAP also sponsored exhibitions and community art centers and produced a historic survey of American design. Renamed the WPA Art Program in 1939.

Federal Emergency Relief Administration (FERA)

A New Deal agency that operated from 1933 to 1935 to oversee public assistance. It funded both direct relief and work relief. The FERA was phased out after the creation of the Works Progress Administration.

Federal Music Project (FMP)

A Works Progress Administration program that employed musicians to perform concerts, teach music classes, and carry out related tasks. Renamed the WPA Music Program in 1939.

Federal One

The division of the Works Progress Administration encompassing the agency's arts projects.

Federal Theatre Project (FTP)

A Works Progress Administration program that produced plays, puppet shows, and circus performances.

Federal Writers' Project (FWP)

A Works Progress Administration program that employed writers to produce guidebooks and to collect and publish historical material, including oral histories, folklore, and traditional ballads. Renamed the WPA Writers' Program in 1939.

FERA

See Federal Emergency Relief Administration (FERA).

Flanagan, Hallie (1890-1969)

Director of the Federal Theatre Project of the Works Progress Administration.

FMP

See Federal Music Project (FMP).

FSA

See Farm Security Administration (FSA).

FTP
See Federal Theatre Project (FTP).

FWP
See Federal Writers Project (FWP).

Great Depression
A worldwide economic crisis lasting from 1929 to the early 1940s and the worst such downturn in the history of the United States.

Hague, Frank (1876-1956)
Democratic power broker and mayor of Jersey City, New Jersey, from 1917 to 1947 who used WPA projects in northern New Jersey to support his political operations.

Harrington, Colonel Francis C. (1887-1940)
Director of the Works Progress Administration from 1938 to 1940.

Hoover, Herbert (1874-1964)
The thirty-first president of the United States, who served from 1929 to 1933.

Hopkins, Harry (1890-1946)
Director of the Works Progress Administration from 1935 to 1938, as well as the Federal Emergency Relief Administration and the Civil Works Administration.

House Un-American Activities Committee (HUAC)
A congressional committee established in 1938 to investigate radical activity. HUAC investigated alleged communist activity in the Works Progress Administration arts programs.

Houseman, John (1902-1988)
Producer, director, and actor who collaborated with Orson Welles on productions for the Federal Theatre Project.

HUAC
See House Un-American Activities Committee (HUAC).

Hundred days
A term applied to the period between March and June 1933, during which the newly installed Roosevelt administration introduced numerous pieces

of legislation and implemented many broad-ranging reforms to address the social and economic woes of the Great Depression.

Ickes, Harold (1874-1952)

Secretary of the Interior and head of the Public Works Administration during the Roosevelt administration.

Keynes, John Maynard (1883-1946)

British economist who argued that governments could help control the cycle of business activity by using the large-scale expenditure of public money as a means of stimulating economic activity.

Long, Huey (1893-1935)

Louisiana governor and senator who advocated a national plan to redistribute wealth from the affluent to the poor.

Means test

A formal investigation conducted when an individual applied for relief that included a thorough review of his or her financial resources to determine if he or she was deserving of government aid.

National Youth Administration (NYA)

An agency under the direction of the Works Progress Administration from 1935 to 1939. The NYA provided employment, educational assistance, and vocational training for young people ages 16-25.

New Era

A period of sustained economic prosperity in the United States lasting from 1921 to 1929.

New Deal

A term used to refer to the broad range of new government programs and agencies established by the administration of President Franklin D. Roosevelt to promote economic recovery and social reform during the Great Depression.

NYA

See National Youth Administration (NYA).

Patronage

The practice of politicians steering government jobs to specific individuals in return for political support.

Public Works Administration (PWA)

A New Deal agency founded in 1933 to oversee large-scale public-works projects, including dams, bridges, and water systems.

PWA

See Public Works Administration (PWA).

Relief

Public assistance provided to those suffering from economic hardship.

Roosevelt, Franklin D. (1882-1945)

The thirty-second president of the United States, who served from 1933 to 1945.

Roosevelt Recession

An economic downturn extending from 1937 through 1938 that caused increased economic hardship and unemployment after several years of slow improvement.

Second New Deal

A term applied to the reforms carried out by the Roosevelt administration in 1935, which included creation of the Works Progress Administration and the passage of the Social Security Act and the National Labor Relations Act.

Security Wage

The specified pay rate provided to employees of the Works Progress Administration. The security wage was set at a lower level than local pay for comparable work in private industry to give workers an incentive to leave work relief programs for private employment.

Social Security Act

The 1935 law that created a federal system of benefits for senior citizens and other vulnerable members of American society, as well as a system of unemployment insurance to benefit those who lose their jobs.

Socialism

A political, economic, and social system based on government or community-wide ownership of industry, property, and resources rather than private ownership.

Sokoloff, Nikolai (1886-1965)

Director of the Federal Music Project of the Works Progress Administration.

Sponsor

The public entity—in most cases, a city or county government—that requested the Works Progress Administration to undertake a project. The sponsor was expected to pay a portion of the project's costs, often by purchasing materials.

Stock Market Crash of 1929

A severe plunge in the value of publicly traded stocks that took place between October 21 and 29, 1929, and triggered the Great Depression.

Temporary Emergency Relief Administration (TERA)

Founded in 1931 by the State of New York, this was the first state-level relief agency in the United States and a model for later relief efforts undertaken by the federal government.

Tennessee Valley Authority (TVA)

A New Deal Agency founded in 1933 that carried out an extensive program of dam construction to provide electricity, control flooding, and generate jobs in the southeastern United States.

TERA

See Temporary Emergency Relief Administration (TERA).

Thomas, J. Parnell (1895-1970)

U.S. representative from New Jersey and conservative opponent of the New Deal.

Townsend, Francis (1867-1960)

Designer of the Townsend Plan, which called for the creation of a government system to provide monthly payments to senior citizens as a means of aiding the recipients and reviving the economy.

TVA

See Tennessee Valley Authority (TVA).

Welles, Orson (1915-1985)

Director and actor who oversaw several stage productions for the Federal Theatre Project in 1936 and 1937.

Williams, Aubrey (1890-1965)

Director of the National Youth Administration and senior assistant to Harry Hopkins in several New Deal relief agencies.

Woodward, Ellen S. (1887-1971)

Director of the Women's Division of the Works Progress Administration (later renamed the Division of Women's and Professional Projects). She filled a similar role for the Federal Emergency Relief Administration and the Civil Works Administration.

Work Projects Administration (WPA)

The name under which the Works Progress Administration was known from 1939 to 1943.

Work relief

A form of public assistance in which those in need are provided with a job, usually funded by the local, state, or federal government, to help support themselves and their family.

Works Progress Administration (WPA)

A federal agency that operated from 1935 to 1943 to oversee an expansive work relief program during the Great Depression. Its name was changed to the Work Projects Administration in 1939.

WPA

Acronym for the Works Progress Administration from 1935 to 1939 and the Work Projects Administration from 1939 to 1943.

CHRONOLOGY

1921

The U.S. economy begins a period of steady growth that continues for the next eight years, creating abundant employment opportunities and rising stock prices. *See p. 7.*

1927

The annual unemployment rate falls to 1.8 percent, the lowest figure since the World War I era.

1929

The annual unemployment rate stands at 3.2 percent. *See p. 8.*

September 3—The Dow Jones Industrial Average reaches a pre-Depression peak of 381.17. *See p. 7.*

October 21-October 29—A massive stock market crash wipes out the financial investments of millions of Americans and sparks the onset of the Great Depression. *See p. 9.*

1930

The annual unemployment rate jumps to 8.9 percent. *See p. 11.*

January—A report by the Committee for Unemployment Relief states that over four million Americans are unemployed.

June—The Hawley-Smoot Act becomes law, imposing steep tariffs on numerous imported goods. Retaliatory action by foreign governments causes further hardship for U.S. businesses.

December—The Bank of the United States shuts down, beginning a wave of bankruptcies by large financial institutions and adding to a yearly total of more than 1,300 failed banks. *See p. 12.*

1931

The country's annual unemployment rate increases to 16.3 percent. *See p. 11.*

Looting, riots, and protest marches become more common throughout the country. *See p. 22.*

October—The New York Temporary Emergency Relief Administration, the first state relief agency in the nation, is established. Many others are created in the next year.

1932

The nation's annual unemployment rate soars to 24.1 percent. *See p. 11.*

January—The Reconstruction Finance Corporation, a government agency designed to aid distressed financial institutions, is approved by Congress after being backed by President Herbert Hoover. *See p. 18.*

July—The Emergency Relief and Construction Act of 1932 becomes law, marking the federal government's first involvement in relief efforts. *See p. 24.*

July 8—The Dow Jones Industrial Average drops to 41.22, its lowest point of the Great Depression, nearly 90 percent below its peak in 1929.

July 28—U.S. military troops drive the Bonus Expeditionary Forces protestors out of Washington, D.C. *See p. 22.*

November 8—Franklin D. Roosevelt defeats Herbert Hoover in the presidential election. *See p. 25.*

1933

The unemployment rate hits 25.2 percent, the highest rate of joblessness in the nation's history. *See p. 11.*

March 4—Franklin D. Roosevelt is sworn in as the thirty-second president of the United States. *See p. 27.*

April—The Civilian Conservation Corps (CCC) enrolls its first member. In the next three months, its ranks will grow to 300,000. *See p. 32.*

May—The Federal Emergency Relief Administration (FERA) begins operation, providing a greatly increased amount of aid to destitute citizens in the form of direct relief and work relief. *See p. 30.*

May—The Tennessee Valley Authority (TVA) is established and begins an expansive dam-building project that brings new jobs and electrification to the southeastern United States. *See p. 37.*

June—The Public Works Administration (PWA) is established to oversee new government-funded infrastructure projects that are intended to put Americans to work and stimulate economic activity. *See p. 35.*

November—The Civil Works Administration (CWA) is established by executive order, launching an ambitious campaign to employ four million people over the winter months. *See p. 38.*

1934

The annual unemployment rate falls under 22 percent. *See p. 41.*

March—The CWA ceases operation. *See p. 40.*

November—Democrats increase their control over both houses of Congress in the fall elections, promising President Roosevelt strong support in the next legislative session. *See p. 41.*

1935

The nation's annual unemployment rate falls to 20.3 percent.

January 4—President Roosevelt announces his plan to create a vast new federal work relief initiative. *See p. 43.*

April 8—The Emergency Relief Appropriation Act of 1935 is signed into law, enabling the creation of the Works Progress Administration (WPA) and the termination of the Federal Emergency Relief Administration. *See p. 49.*

May 6—The WPA is officially created by executive order, and Harry Hopkins is appointed as its director. *See p. 50.*

December—The WPA has 2.6 million Americans on its payroll.

1936

The annual unemployment rate decreases to 17 percent.

February—The WPA work force tops 3 million for the first time, but hiring drops in the following months. The agency's work force averages about 2.5 million for the year.

June—WPA crews begin construction of the Timberline Lodge in Oregon. *See p. 65.*

November 3—President Roosevelt wins reelection, and Democrats increase their majorities in both houses of Congress. *See p. 89.*

1937

The annual unemployment rate falls to 14 percent.

President Roosevelt pursues his unsuccessful "court-packing" plan to increase the number of Supreme Court justices. *See p. 90.*

The WPA begins construction of LaGuardia Airport in New York City. *See p. 66.*

January—WPA workers assist in providing emergency services following devastating flooding along the Ohio and Mississippi Rivers. *See p. 68.*

June—The Federal Theatre Project musical *The Cradle Will Rock* is prevented from opening in New York City. In response, the theatrical company stages an unauthorized performance. *See p. 77.*

Summer—The WPA work force is drastically reduced, reaching a low of 1.4 million in September, as President Roosevelt decides to reduce federal expenditures on relief. The cutbacks lead to protests and strikes, particularly among members of the arts programs. *See p. 91.*

Fall—An economic downturn dubbed the "Roosevelt Recession" takes root, causing a decline in business productivity and a new surge in unemployment. *See p. 91.*

1938

The annual unemployment rate jumps to 19.1 percent.

February—The size of the WPA work force surges back over the two-million mark.

April—President Roosevelt requests an additional $3 billion in relief funding, which results in a further expansion of WPA hiring in the following months. *See p. 92.*

May—The House Un-American Activities Committee is established. In hearings that continue until December, the committee investigates allegations that WPA arts programs have been infiltrated by communists. *See p. 94.*

September—A massive hurricane slams the Northeast and WPA work crews assist in the disaster response.

November—The WPA work force reaches its all-time peak, with 3.3 million Americans on the payroll. *See p. 92.*

November—Riding a downturn in public support for Roosevelt's New Deal, Republicans pick up seats in both the House and Senate in the fall elections. *See p. 96.*

December—Harry Hopkins leaves the WPA to become the secretary of commerce. Colonel Francis C. Harrington is appointed as the new director of the WPA.

1939

The nation's annual unemployment rate drops to 17.2 percent.

The Works Progress Administration is renamed the Work Projects Administration as part of a reorganization of the executive branch of the federal government. As part of the same reform, the National Youth Administration is removed from the WPA to become part of the Federal Security Agency. *See p. 98.*

April—The number of people employed by the WPA drops to 2.7 million. The reduction continues in the following months, resulting in an average work force of about 2.3 million for the year.

June—The Emergency Relief Appropriation Act of 1939 becomes law. It mandates extensive reforms to the WPA, including a reduction in funding, changes in hiring and work regulations, and the reorganization of the arts programs. *See p. 97.*

September—German forces invade Poland, beginning World War II. *See p. 99.*

November—President Roosevelt's "cash and carry" policy is approved by Congress, allowing the United States to sell armaments to Great Britain. *See p. 99.*

1940

The annual unemployment rate in the United States falls to 14.6 percent.

May—The WPA work force is reduced to 1.9 million. It will never again exceed 2 million. *See p. 101.*

June—The WPA increases its involvement in national defense projects, a trend that will continue until the agency ceases operations in 1943. *See p. 100.*

July—Women begin taking part in WPA vocational training to prepare for jobs in defense industries. *See p. 101.*

November—Franklin Roosevelt is elected to a third term as president.

December—President Roosevelt states that the nation must become "the great arsenal of democracy" to oppose the Axis Powers.

1941

The annual unemployment rate falls to 9.9 percent.

March—President Roosevelt signs the Lend-Lease bill into law, allowing the United States to provide armaments and other material to Great Britain and, later, to China and the Soviet Union.

July—The number of WPA workers is cut by more than 350,000 in the span of one month, to just over 1 million in total.

December 7—Japanese forces attack the U.S. naval base at Pearl Harbor in Hawaii. The following day, the United States officially enters World War II. *See p. 102.*

1942

The annual unemployment rate falls to 4.7 percent.

The National Resources Planning Board recommends the establishment of a permanent federal work agency to oversee public employment programs, but its recommendation is never acted upon. *See p. 111.*

March—The WPA work force drops below 1 million for the first time since October 1935.

August—The number of WPA employees dips to 447,000.

December 4—President Roosevelt announces that the WPA will cease operation the following year. At month's end, the agency's payroll is just under 337,000. *See p. 102.*

1943

The nation's annual unemployment rate drops to 1.9 percent.

June 30—The WPA ceases operation. A total of 42,437 people collect paychecks from the agency in its final month of existence. *See p. 102.*

1945

April 12—President Roosevelt dies, and Harry S. Truman succeeds him as president.

May 7—The last German military forces surrender, ending World War II in Europe.

August 6—The United States drops the first of two atomic bombs on the nation of Japan. The first bomb destroys the city of Hiroshima, and the second bomb, delivered on August 9, hits Nagasaki.

August 14—Japan formally surrenders, bringing World War II to an end.

1961

President John F. Kennedy creates the Peace Corps by executive order. While it provides employment to those who enroll, it functions more as an international service initiative than a jobs program. About 7,000 people join the corps in its first two years.

1962

March—President Kennedy signs the Manpower Development and Training Act of 1962, establishing a government-sponsored job-training program. *See p. 113.*

1964

August—The Economic Opportunity Act of 1964 is signed by President Lyndon B. Johnson. It establishes a range of employment and job-training programs, including the Neighborhood Youth Corps, the Job Corps, and the Federal Work-Study Program. *See p. 113.*

1965

The National Foundation on the Arts and the Humanities Act of 1965 becomes law, establishing the National Endowment for the Arts and the National Endowment for the Humanities—the first major federal agencies providing funding for the arts since the Great Depression. *See p. 111.*

1973

December—President Richard M. Nixon signs the Comprehensive Employment and Training Act (CETA), which provides federal funds to states for use in job training and publicly managed employment programs. *See p. 113.*

1977

CETA is expanded during the administration of President Jimmy Carter. It becomes the most expansive federally funded jobs program since the WPA, providing jobs to 742,000 people at its peak in 1978. *See p. 113.*

1996

President Bill Clinton signs welfare reform legislation that establishes the Temporary Assistance for Needy Families (TANF) program, which creates the framework for state-run welfare-to-work initiatives. *See p. 114.*

2008

November 4—Barack Obama is elected president as the nation faces one of its most extreme economic recessions since the 1930s. *See p. 114.*

2009

February 17—President Obama signs the American Recovery and Reinvestment Act into law. *See p. 114.*

SOURCES FOR FURTHER STUDY

Franklin D. Roosevelt Presidential Library and Museum. Retrieved from http://www.fdrlibrary
.marist.edu/. The library and museum's World Wide Web site provides access to a vast
range of its archival materials on Franklin and Eleanor Roosevelt, including photos, documents, audio recordings, and film footage.

Ginzberg, Eli. *The Unemployed.* Edited by Ben B. Seligman. New Brunswick, NJ: Transaction,
2004. Based on interviews with 200 New York City families who received work relief
and direct relief, this book offers a thorough study of the personal effects of joblessness
and government assistance efforts during the Great Depression.

Kennedy, Roger G., and David Larkin. *When Art Worked: The New Deal, Art, and Democracy.*
New York: Random House, 2009. This large-format art book chronicles the influence of
the Works Progress Administration and other New Deal initiatives on American art and
culture. This work is especially notable for its beautiful reproductions of Depression-era
paintings, prints, and photographs.

Leuchtenburg, William Edward. *The FDR Years: On Roosevelt and His Legacy.* New York:
Columbia University Press, 1995. This insightful collection of essays provides a
detailed examination of President Roosevelt's character and philosophy of government
and discusses his influence on American history.

McElvaine, Robert S., ed. *Down and Out in the Great Depression: Letters from the "Forgotten
Man."* Chapel Hill, NC: University of North Carolina Press, 1983. This work collects
letters of criticism and gratitude written by Americans to President Roosevelt during
the Great Depression.

"A New Deal for the Arts." National Archives. Retrieved from http://www.archives.gov/exhibits
/new_deal_for_the_arts/. This Web site was created from a U.S. National Archives exhibit on the arts projects of the Roosevelt administration. It includes reproductions of art-
works, photographs, and posters from the era.

New Deal Network. Retrieved from http://newdeal.feri.org/aaccc/index.htm. This online
educational guide offers photographs, articles, speeches, lessons plans, and other
materials related to the various New Deal programs of the Roosevelt administration.

Sherwood, Robert E. *Roosevelt and Hopkins: An Intimate History.* New York: Harper, 1950.
Reprint, New York: Enigma, 2008. This book, written by a New Deal insider, offers a

classic account of the working relationship between Harry Hopkins and Franklin D. Roosevelt. The first portion of the book covers their work in the 1930s, when Hopkins headed the Works Progress Administration and other relief agencies.

Taylor, Nick. *American Made: The Enduring Legacy of the WPA: When FDR Put the Nation to Work.* New York: Bantam, 2008. This engaging history of the Works Progress Administration includes accounts of individuals who were employed in various WPA work projects.

Watkins, T. H. *The Hungry Years: A Narrative History of the Great Depression in America.* New York: Holt, 1999. Watkins provides a thorough and very readable chronicle of the Great Depression and the government's efforts to respond to the crisis.

WPA Today. Available online at http://www.wpatoday.org. This Web site provides a broad range of information about the Works Progress Administration, with a particular focus on WPA-built projects that are still in existence.

BIBLIOGRAPHY

Books

Bindas, Kenneth J. *Remembering the Great Depression in the Rural South*. Gainesville: University of Florida Press, 2007.

Brands, H. W. *Traitor to His Class: The Privileged Life and Radical Presidency of Franklin Delano Roosevelt*. New York: Doubleday, 2008.

Brock, William R. *Welfare, Democracy, and the New Deal*. Cambridge, UK: Cambridge University Press, 1988.

Cohen, Robert, ed. *Dear Mrs. Roosevelt: Letters from Children of the Great Depression*. Chapel Hill: University of North Carolina Press, 2002.

DiNunzio, Mario R. *Franklin D. Roosevelt and the Third American Revolution*. Santa Barbara, CA: Praeger, 2011.

Edsforth, Ronald. *The New Deal: America's Response to the Great Depression*. Malden, MA: Blackwell, 2000.

Final Report on the WPA Program 1935-43. Washington, DC: U.S. Government Printing Office, 1947.

Folsom, Burton W. *New Deal or Raw Deal: How FDR's Economic Legacy Has Damaged America*. New York: Threshold Editions, 2008.

Ginzberg, Eli. *The Unemployed*. Edited by Ben B. Seligman. New Brunswick, NJ: Transaction, 2004.

Hamby, Alonzo L. *For the Survival of Democracy: Franklin Roosevelt and the World Crisis of the 1930s*. New York: Free Press, 2004.

Hiltzik, Michael. *The New Deal: A Modern History*. New York: Free Press, 2011.

Hopkins, June. *Harry Hopkins: Sudden Hero, Brash Reformer*. New York: St. Martin's, 1999.

Kennedy, Roger G., and David Larkin. *When Art Worked: The New Deal, Art, and Democracy*. New York: Random House, 2009.

Lawson, Alan. *A Commonwealth of Hope: The New Deal Response to Crisis*. Baltimore, MD: Johns Hopkins University Press, 2006.

Lebergott, Stanley. *Manpower in Economic Growth: The American Record since 1800*. New York: McGraw-Hill, 1964.

Leuchtenburg, William E. *The FDR Years: On Roosevelt and His Legacy.* New York: Columbia University Press, 1995.

Leuchtenburg, William E., ed. *The New Deal: A Documentary History.* Columbia: University of South Carolina Press, 1968.

Louchheim, Katie, ed. *The Making of the New Deal: The Insiders Speak.* Cambridge, MA: Harvard University Press, 1983.

McElvaine, Robert S. *Down and Out in the Great Depression: Letters from the Forgotten Man.* Chapel Hill: University of North Carolina Press, 1983.

McKinzie, Richard D. *The New Deal for Artists.* Princeton, NJ: Princeton University Press, 1973.

O'Connor, Francis V. *The New Deal Art Projects: An Anthology of Memoirs.* Washington, DC: Smithsonian Institution Press, 1972.

Roosevelt, Franklin D. *The Public Papers and Addresses of Franklin D. Roosevelt.* 13 vols. New York: Russell & Russell, 1969.

Rose, Nancy E. *Put to Work: Relief Programs in the Great Depression.* New York: Monthly Review Press, 1994.

Security, Work, and Relief Policies: Report of the Committee on Long-Range Work and Relief Policies to the National Resources Planning Board. Washington, DC: U.S. Government Printing Office, 1942, p. 247.

Sherwood, Robert E. *Roosevelt and Hopkins: An Intimate History.* New York: Harper, 1950. Reprint, New York: Enigma, 2008.

Shlaes, Amity. *The Forgotten Man: A New History of the Great Depression.* New York: HarperCollins, 2007.

Sitkoff, Harvard, ed. *Fifty Years Later: The New Deal Evaluated.* New York: Knopf, 1985.

Taylor, Nick. *American-Made: The Enduring Legacy of the WPA: When FDR Put the Nation to Work.* New York: Bantam, 2008.

Terkel, Studs. *Hard Times: An Oral History of the Great Depression.* New York: Pantheon, 1986.

Trattner, Walter I. *From Poor Law to Welfare State: A History of Social Welfare in America.* 2nd ed. New York: Free Press, 1979.

Watkins, T. H. *The Hungry Years: A Narrative History of the Great Depression in America.* New York: Holt, 1999.

Periodicals

Bristol, Margaret C. "Personal Reactions of Assignees to W.P.A. in Chicago." *Social Service Review* 12 (1), March 1938, pp. 69-100.

Golway, Terry. "W.P.A. Projects Left Their Stamp on the Region." *New York Times*, April 15, 2009, p. NJ1.

Grabell, Michael. "How Not to Revive an Economy." *New York Times*, February 12, 2012, p. SR8.

Online Resources

Brown, Lorraine. "Federal Theatre: Melodrama, Social Protest, and Genius," n.d. American Memory Collection, Library of Congress. Retrieved from http://memory.loc.gov/am mem/fedtp/ftbrwn00.html.

"Franklin D. Roosevelt's Fireside Chats." American Presidency Project. Retrieved from http://www.presidency.ucsb.edu/fireside.php.

McKee, Brent. WPA Today website. Retrieved from http://www.wpatoday.org/Home_Page.html .

"A New Deal for the Arts." U.S. National Archives and Records Administration. Retrieved from http://www.archives.gov/exhibits/new_deal_for_the_arts/.

Noah, Timothy. "CBO, Meet CWA," *Slate,* January 27, 2009. Retrieved from http://www.slate .com/articles/news_and_politics/chatterbox/2009/01/cbo_meet_cwa.html.

DVD

American Experience: FDR. PBS, 1994.

American Experience: The Civilian Conservation Corps. PBS, 2009.

American Experience: The Crash of 1929. PBS, 1990.

The Dust Bowl: A Film by Ken Burns, Episode 2. PBS, 2012.

PHOTO AND ILLUSTRATION CREDITS

Chapter Five: Prints & Photographs Division, Library of Congress, LC-USZ62-25812 (p. 72); Louisiana Division/City Archives, New Orleans Public Library (p. 74); Courtesy of the Special Collections Department, University of Iowa (p. 75); Photograph by Dorothea Lange, FSA/OWI Black-and-White Negatives Collection, Prints & Photographs Division, Library of Congress, LC-DIG-fsa-8b29516 (p. 76); Photofest (p. 78); Harris & Ewing Collection, Prints & Photographs Division, Library of Congress, LC-DIG-hec-25609 (p. 81); National Archives, NWDNS-179-WP-1563 (p. 82); Photograph by Gordon Parks, FSA/OWI Black-and-White Negatives Collection, Prints & Photographs Division, Library of Congress, LC-USW3-014897-C (p. 84).

Chapter Six: AP Photo/CH (p. 90); Bain Collection, Prints & Photographs Division, Library of Congress, LC-USZ62-119504 (p. 93); Harris & Ewing Collection, Prints & Photographs Division, Library of Congress, LC-DIG-hec-22503 (p. 95); Prints & Photographs Division, Library of Congress, LC-USZ62-45642 (p. 100).

Chapter Seven: Prints & Photographs Division, Library of Congress, HABS ORE, 3-GOCA.V, 1-6 (p. 106); Louisiana Division/City Archives, New Orleans Public Library (p. 108); Artist: Charles Santore, 2009 National Book Festival Poster, Courtesy Library of Congress (http://www.loc.gov/bookfest/kids-teachers/hostyourown/poster.html) (p. 110); Courtesy, Corporation for National and Community Service (p. 112); Official White House Photo by Lawrence Jackson (p. 116).

Biographies: Van Vechten Collection, Prints & Photographs Division, Library of Congress, LC-USZ62-42476 (p. 121); Harris & Ewing Collection, Prints & Photographs Division, Library of Congress, LC-DIG-hec-25582 (p. 125); © Photo12 / The Image Works (p. 129); Prints & Photographs Division, Library of Congress, LC-USZ62-94417 (p. 133); Martha Holmes/Time Life Pictures/Getty Images (p. 141); Courtesy of the Franklin D. Roosevelt Digital Archives (p. 145); Photofest (p. 150); Harris & Ewing Collection, Prints & Photographs Division, Library of Congress, LC-DIG-hec-25608 (p. 154).

INDEX